NOTTINGHAM'S FAMILY FIRST 1965-2005

Forty years' practical work with local people overcoming difficulties

by Ruth I Johns

founder of Family First

The cover photo is from the cover of a Family First information pack (1995) and shows children playing outside at the Croft Family Centre day nursery

First published by Family First Limited
in 2006

A catalogue record for this book is available from the British Library

ISBN 0 9550948 0 1

Printed by Warwick Printing Co Ltd

Family First Limited
375 Alfred Street North
Nottingham
NG3 1AA
www.familyfirst.org.uk

Order direct from the distributor PO Box 66 Warwick CV34 4XE £10 (plus £1.50 p & p UK), from bookshops or www.Amazon.co.uk. Or ask for it at your local library

To the thousands of people who have been part of the
Family First story over the past 40 years

Contents

Foreword

As Chair of family **first,** it gives me pleasure to write the foreword for this book, written to celebrate the fortieth anniversary of this unique organisation. family **first** was established in 1965 and its first project was to address the specific housing and support needs of young single mothers, both unmarried mothers and deserted wives.

It takes courage and determination to set up any organisation. It takes even more courage and determination to set one up that goes against the status quo. Ruth I Johns had both in abundance. She succeeded in setting up an organisation that continues to deliver services to local people in a way that challenges the status quo.

This book not only charts the history of family **first** and its work over the past forty years: it also puts on record the work of thousands of people involved as tenants, service users, staff, volunteers, students and trainees in a myriad of different, often imaginative and successful ways. All of them have worked towards the common purpose of finding local solutions to local problems and needs.

We commissioned Ruth I Johns to write this book for us, not as the founder of family **first**, but for her skill and expertise as a community historian. With this perspective, she has been able to take a reflective look over the past forty years and chart its progress within an historical context of growing regulation for regulation's sake and how this has helped, but more often hindered, the growth and development of the organisation over the years.

Nottinghamshire County Council held a Family First 40th anniversary reception at County Hall in 2005. Left to right: Janet Butler, Chair of Family First; Ruth Johns, founder; Councillor Mrs Nellie Smedley, Chairman of Nottinghamshire County Council, and Ann Cartwright, Chief Executive of Family First. Nottingham City Council also held a reception to celebrate 40 years of Family First.

Today, more than ever before, social policy is being developed and driven by central government. It often prevents small community based organisations like family **first** from developing and delivering a local solution to a local problem in the innovative ways we have done in the past. In the current climate, as a small organisation, family **first** needs to find a new way to develop and grow, whilst at the same time protecting its legacy.

One solution is to form an alliance with a larger organisation that shares our values, ethos and beliefs. We believe that we have found this with the LHA-ASRA[1] Group and are currently working towards developing a strategic alliance with them. The name of family **first** will be preserved along with its commitment to finding local solutions for local problems. Within the alliance we will be able to create opportunities to develop and grow all our services in a way that would have been impossible as a stand-alone organisation. It gives us a new lease of life and a real opportunity to continue to develop innovative and imaginative services for local people for another forty years and beyond. As they say "Life begins at Forty" and we believe that this is our new beginning.

I hope you will enjoy reading our history over the last forty years and that it gives you some insights into the ups and downs of developing and managing a small community based organisation. I also hope that it might encourage you to become involved in our work. If so, you can find out how by visiting our website at www.familyfirst.org.uk.

Janet Butler
Chair of family **first**
December 2005

[1] Leicester Housing Association-ASRA. ASRA is Urdu for 'shelter', and is the name of a housing association linked to LHA

Soon after The Croft opened, this small office extension was built to cope with the large demand for Family First's help. The Croft remained Family First's administrative base for more than three decades. The open front door led to the Reception office on the left and the large Community Room on the right. A coin telephone in the lobby was used by neighbours and tenants. See chapter on Neighbourhood Centres

AIMING FOR PRACTICAL JUSTICE

Family First, Nottingham, was founded late in 1965. Immediately, it started to find homes for homeless families and individuals and soon established its own innovative housing project for young lone mothers in Alexandra Park, Nottingham. Family First created neighbourhood centres; opportunities for people to meet, to socialise and to learn; a day nursery and a wide range of family support services; a furniture and clothing service including shops, and training opportunities. This book is the story of what Family First has achieved; what it is now undertaking; the problems it has encountered, and its legacy. Family First has had an influence far beyond its work in Nottingham.

Family First's work over four decades is a rich story of both continuity and change: changing times but continuing needs. It is the story of a multi-faceted local organisation, which is variously described as ***'holistic'***, ***'flexible'***, or ***"filling a gaping hole in services for people in need."*** By officials in statutory departments, it has often been described as ***"a one-off that cannot be categorised."***

Background to the founding of Family First

Through the experiences of life and work, I became curious about social issues and grew into a pragmatic problem solver. I had no urge to be a pioneer. But I became determined to try to help to provide opportunity for families and for young people stigmatised and stereotyped because of their circumstances, often before they reached adulthood. I was angry how easily young people, including lone parents, were categorised as ***'beyond hope'***.

I wrote the founding document of Family First early in 1965[1]. I was 31. Family First started later that year in Alexandra Park, Nottingham, where it was to have its pioneer non-institutional housing project for young lone mothers and its offices, and later a Family Centre and 14 new flats. Very quickly, the concepts of the founding document took a tangible form. I was surprised when the Home Office stated: ***"Your project is a revolutionary idea."***

Family First's ability to respond to real needs has attracted many to its ranks for four decades. For example, Dolores Williams, Family First Service Manager (Housing), told me in 2005: ***"I have worked for Family First since 2003 after eight years with another housing association. I like Family First's various projects and how they come together to help people."***

I was Family First's Director for over 10 years. My family was the voluntary resident family in its housing project in Alexandra Park. In July 1976, I moved to London and was adviser to Family First until mid-1978.

Nearly three decades later, as a community historian living several days a week back in Nottingham, I was asked by Ann Cartwright to write Family First's history[2]. It was a challenge to research what happened under Angus Walker's watch (1976-1988), that of Graham Wright (1988-1997) and Ann Cartwright (1997 -). At the end of 2004, I became President of Family First.

In the intervening decades, I continued to work in the field of community self-help and came to know 13 UK cities well, with their different strengths, traditions and problems. I learned how difficult it was for successful locally appropriate projects and social enterprises to retain their autonomy.

---

1 The 1975 reaffirmed version appears below. The longer original version is in *Life Goes On* (see next footnote)

2 The Gulbenkian Foundation asked me to write a book about the first decade of Family First. It was published as *Life Goes On* in 1982 and offers detail about the practice, and especially the philosophy, of Family First's early years. For full details see Backlist on www.plowrightpress.co.uk . In this 40-year history, I have not repeated much from *Life Goes On* because anyone interested can get it from a library or purchase it. Its 1982 style looks dated but the information is accurate

From 1976-1983, I was often an advocate on their behalf to central Government, local authorities and the business sector.

In 1984, a medical injury paralysed me and turned my life upside down. Mobility slowly returned. But, needing a physically calmer life than formerly, I became a community historian. Too often history is written from the top down. Becoming a community historian was a different approach to communicating, especially about people and organisations at local level. Therefore, I have written this history as a community historian, not as founder of Family First.

It is important here to state the power of myth! British history leads us to believe stereotypes of the instigators of social change. The role that 'ordinary' people play in their local communities to create positive social change is often acknowledged with little more than lip-service by those who wield power. Thus it was that, although I started Family First with absolutely no personal history of wealth, it somehow became part of the story of Family First that I came from a privileged background!

'Ordinary' people can and often do achieve social change even when they have no wealth or heredity advantage. But, often, it is not the true story that gets recorded. For example, Patte Wheat and Leonard Lieber wrote[3]: ***"Family First Trust was founded and directed for ten years by Ruth Johns, a journalist from a wealthy, prominent family. It is headquartered in Ruth's original home ..."*** This myth has been reiterated over and over in books, articles and, sometimes, even within Family First. For instance, in a brief introductory history in Family First's Three Year Plan 1997-2000 was written: ***"Ruth Johns provided the first supported housing project from her own house at The Croft."***

In 1965, the Johns family purchased Mayholme in Alexandra Park with a mortgage after selling its house. This was agreed with Family First's Management Committee as a device to get started before it had finance to purchase the adjoining property (The Croft) with large grounds. The owners agreed to sell The Croft to Family First if it raised the funds within six months. It did. Our purchase of Mayholme was conditional upon our selling it on for the same price to Family First. That all happened very quickly. And, for many years, Family First's property in Alexandra Park was known as The Croft, whereas in later years the name Mayholme became more widely used, which is why I usually refer to Mayholme/The Croft.

Outline of the early history

Despite availability of accurate information, serious mistakes have been made along the way with Family First's history. For example, its 25th Anniversary Annual Report 1990/91 stated that it registered as a housing association in 1974. Wrong! It was a registered housing association from 1966.

The various strands of Family First's work evolved quickly in response to local needs. Within 18 months, Family First rehabilitated and converted Mayholme/The Croft for its administrative base and a project where young lone mums lived whilst pregnant and sorting out their own and their baby's future. These were times when most young lone mums without family support had their babies adopted. There was little and, often, no alternative. Land on the site was earmarked for a family centre and building of more homes.

Even before the project opened, Family First (working from a room in Mayholme) was inundated with requests to help families in crisis. The requests came from Local Authority social workers, probation officers, hospital social workers, doctors, voluntary organisations and, often, self-referrals. Little existing help was available in Nottingham for the people referred but, as the letter from the Town Clerk below illustrates, this was not officially acknowledged. Many of the families needing help were deserted wives with children. This was the time when Nottingham, like many other cities, was experiencing wholesale demolition of homes in its central districts.

From the start, Family First was finding homes for people in and around

[3] In *Hope for the Children* [Winston Press Inc. USA. 1979]

Nottingham. Networks of volunteers quickly undertook myriads of different tasks.

Social workers were asking for Family First's help with clothing, furniture and especially warm bedding for their clients. Many were struggling in accommodation compulsorily purchased by the Local Authority prior to demolition within months/years. Planning blight meant the properties were in bad repair. Many children spent important growing-up years in 'condemned housing[4]'. Family First was soon running an organised Furniture and Clothing Service and shops.

"***Family First was my lifeline for helping some young mothers,***" Kamla Joashi told me (2005). Aged 19, Kamla Joashi came to England alone from India in 1954 determined to train for nursing before advancing to midwifery. She was the first Asian District Midwife in the city before becoming a Health Visitor in central areas. ***"I asked Family First for help when there was real need. It meant so much for the young mothers to have some beautiful clothes, including hand-knitted for their babies. Conditions at that time could be bad."*** Kamla Joashi asked for this help soon after Family First started. She later became a member of Family First's Management Committee.

Links with Mapperley [Psychiatric] Hospital developed and led to some patients spending part of their day outside the hospital engaged in creative/educational activities at the back of one of Family First's shops nearby. This developed into a well-run pop-in workshop which typified Family First's long association with people with mental health issues.

These were some of the various strands of Family First's activities that wove a holistic service. People, through self-help and opportunity, improved, built or rebuilt their lives. The most distinctive thing about Family First was its strong belief in people's ability to move positively forward in life with some appropriate and timely practical assistance.

Family First was soon asked to accept trainee social workers on placement and the culture shock they experienced was often profound. The same was true of many who came as volunteers.

"In a strange way, I grew up with Family First. It was the first opportunity I had to be an individual rather than a daughter and a wife/mother. It helped me accept my competence as well as the need for group support in times of stress.

"I well remember times when Muriel [Sutherland] and Sue [French] gathered in the office for coffee when I was a new volunteer. Their acceptance then made it possible for me to try more new fields . . . it helped me through a very bad patch. I think it was your insistence that everyone had talents that helped everyone, and blurred the lines between helper and helped. Certainly I keep that knowledge close to me in my present work . .

"My work with the Department of Child Psychiatry keeps me continually stretched. I have started lecturing to health visitors, home helps and residential social workers . . ." wrote LE (1976). She took professional training following several years volunteering with Family First.

The importance of gaining skills was always of key importance within Family First. It still is.

All members of the early Management Committee had relevant skills (not necessarily professional ones) and were willing to be involved in a practical way in the organisation. The Committee included a solicitor, P G Hebbert, and an accountant, C E Akeroyd, who gave invaluable time and skill in the early years. They were bold in affirming Family First's values and their skills helped to ensure its probity. They were, for example, helpful in supporting appropriate action when, in the early days, an architect started to spend above an agreed budget without authorisation.

Whilst researching this book, it became evident that the founding document that set out Family First's beliefs has stood the test of time. Time and again, it is referred to in the archives and in conversation. For example,

[4] The story of the compulsory demolition of 340 acres of St Ann's (uprooting 30,000 people) is told in my book *St Ann's Nottingham: inner-city voices*. See www.plowrightpress.co.uk

one former Family First Manager told me (2005) that he keeps a copy of the updated 1975 version in his desk drawer in his current place of work. The text is below:-

Aims and Objectives of Family First Trust

Family First Trust's legal status as a registered Voluntary Housing Association and a Charity enables it to provide housing and other practical help (except financial) for families and individuals who are in need.

The Management Committee states the following as its policy:-

- Family First should remain a local and a community based organisation. It attaches much importance to enabling self-help.
- Family First works for people of any race, colour or creed, and accepts that everyone belongs to a family. It aims to prevent crises developing into long-term problems.
- Family First's only long-term material aim is to own a substantial number of housing units available for rent to meet urgent housing need. The number owned must be no greater than that which can effectively be managed in a direct, personal and non-bureaucratic way.
- Family First should evolve ways of enabling tenants/neighbours/helpers to live full, creative lives and should encourage participation in its community work (e.g. Croft Family Centre).
- Family First should not necessarily aim to retain control of any venture it pioneers. Sometimes it can work as a catalyst in a new situation until the usefulness of a venture is established and can be run without its help.
- In the housing field, Family First can create far more homes than those for which it retains ownership and direct management.
- Family First supports its staff and volunteers in their role of workers with definite aims, and discourages use of time spent on 'representative' committees without clear objectives.
- Family First recognises the value of informed opinion and accepts responsibility for documenting experimental work so that its successes and failures can help others.
- Family First sets itself a high standard of management efficiency and an economical use of resources. All members of the Management Committee have an active interest in the work of Family First. The Committee should regularly reassess the value and direction of the work of Family First in the light of changing needs and changing resources.
- Family First respects the right of all people to a home, privacy, peace and a place in their local neighbourhood or community. Family First tenants have a right to these things on equal, but not special, terms. To treat any group, or individual, as basically 'different' simply because they are in some kind of need or have a particular problem or handicap is to degrade them, to use them and ultimately to destroy their self-respect. All work done by Family First should enable people to make their own decisions whenever possible, and to accept responsibility for those decisions.

But it was a struggle!

After consultations with Nottingham's statutory services before it started, Family First believed there would be mutual co-operation. However, whilst statutory bodies asked Family First to assist their clients in increasing numbers, the City Council failed to recognise that co-operation. Even when the City Estates Surveyor's Department suggested that Family First should negotiate to purchase a plot of land in Thyra Grove at the back of The Croft (1966), the City Council refused consent. The site would have created direct access between Family First's developing neighbourhood base in Alexandra Park and the City Council's planned Caunton Avenue housing estate. Residents on that unhappy housing complex, which was pulled down in 1994, might well have benefited from the link.

Eventually, I made public reference to how much Family First was achieving ***"in spite of rather than because of the Council"***. Alderman Mrs Joan Case broke ranks (at first asking that her visit was not publicised). She was the first councillor who came to see what Family First was doing. As a result, she agreed to open Family First's Garden Party at The Croft in June 1968, which was brave just after the Council had refused Family First a loan of £35,000 to build the planned 14 two-storey flats on land at The Croft. She publicly said she realised ***"how much distressed people need the services given by Family First"***.

William Whitlock MP asked the Town Clerk why the City Council refused the loan. He replied: ***"I am sure Family First Trust are enthusiastic and anxious to expand their services quickly, but the proposals for the flats and day nursery are a little too ambitious, and I would have thought the Trust would be better advised to increase their activities by stages when they have concrete evidence from their own experience of the demand for the service they wish to provide."*** The evidence was abundant. But there was deep seated prejudice behind such decisions. However, social workers would seek Family First's help, unavailable elsewhere, for their clients and ask us not to report this to their Director. He had been directed to tell his staff not to use Family First's services.

To be fair, from the start Nottingham City Housing Department recognised Family First's value as support for its own work and offered co-operation as we shall see later in the Housing chapter.

Like many organisations today, Family First is involved in arrangements (often called service level agreements) and short-term funding contracts, and is thus 'partnered' with a range of statutory and other bodies. For the historian, it is hard to follow a chronological 'paper trail' of events: for example, to link frequent changes of Government policy to how, via other bodies including local authorities, they precisely have an impact on a voluntary organisation's ability to deliver its own (or Government) policies at the grass roots.

For instance, each change in governments' methods of underpinning basic family income alters the practicalities between Family First and its tenants and other service users. Which families can use its day nursery? How is that decided in relation to how a day nursery place is paid for? Can that decision be made by Family First to meet its tenants'/users' needs, or is it made by statutory bodies which fund a specific number of places to meet some of their objectives? Is it possible to have a practical mutually agreed policy? Local government reorganisation has happened twice during Family First's four decades, the City Council becoming a Unitary Authority again in 1998. For Family First, the decades working directly with Nottinghamshire County Council were more positive: its relationship with the voluntary sector was creative and open.

Family First is challenged to continue to exist as an independent local organisation within the regulatory and social policy climate in which it now has to operate. It has striven for 40 years to remain of a size to enable it to be locally appropriate and practical, and to evolve dynamically. It has occasionally fallen down on the high standards it sets itself, and this short history is no whitewash. It is significant that, when mistakes have occurred, they have been quickly and efficiently corrected in areas where there is no imposed regulation of its administration! Imposed regulation can interfere with effective management.

"It sometimes feels that 50% of senior managers' time is taken up dealing with regulatory processes, 30% finding their way around ever-changing funding routes so the work can continue and 20% left to do the job that motivated them to want to do it in the first place." Ann Cartwright, Chief Executive (2004).

About the research

Like many organisations, Family First has incomplete archives. Nevertheless, a large collection of papers (many unsorted) built up in The Croft cellar. These archives were brought up, boxed and put at my disposal in 2004. There had obviously been periodic clear-outs. I searched for the archives most likely to be helpful for this book. These filled my office!

Useful sources for this history have been interviews or discussions with staff, service users and others who have known Family First at different times over 40 years. Some I have been unable to contact, for example, the third Director, Graham Wright. I have seen minutes, annual reports, newsletters, reports about specific parts of Family First's work, discussion documents concerning proposals for developing projects or assessing their effectiveness. A letter in the *Nottingham Evening Post* asked people to write in with recollections.

I was given freedom by the current Chief Executive, Ann Cartwright, and members of the Family First Board to determine the content of this book.

Family First was established as Family First Trust. In 1966, it registered as a housing association called the Alexandra Park Housing Association Ltd. It also registered under the Industrial and Provident Societies Act 1965. Following the Housing Act 1974, it registered with the Housing Corporation in 1975. The Charities Act 1992 necessitated a change in registration to a limited company, whilst remaining a charity incorporated as an industrial and provident society. So Family First Limited was born. This explains why the governing body changed from a Management Committee to a Board. The name in everyday use has always been Family First, more recently designed as family **first**.

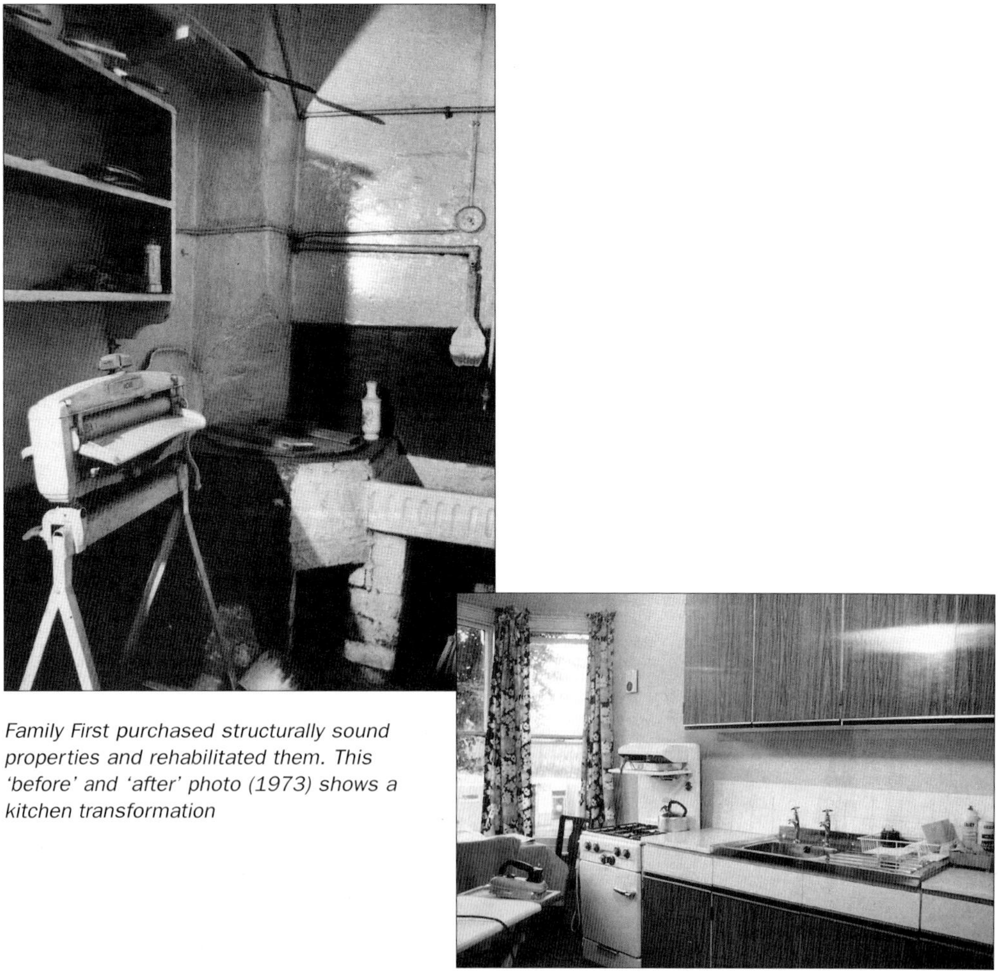

Family First purchased structurally sound properties and rehabilitated them. This 'before' and 'after' photo (1973) shows a kitchen transformation

Nottingham's Family First 1965-2005 ISBN 09550948 01

HOUSING

In 2005, Family First provided 386 affordable homes for over 1,200 people in Nottingham and surrounding districts. Tenants are single people, couples and families of all ages. Most accommodation is independent. Some has back-up support. Family First's housing aims have been increasingly frustrated in recent times by imposed policies that assume it should develop as a larger general purpose housing association rather than stay as a small specialist one.

Historical context

Family First never set out to become a big housing association and it is not. Housing was intended to be a tool, not its only or necessarily its prime purpose.

Housing would either:-

- assist individuals or families, many of them lone-parent families at a time of crisis in their lives when they urgently needed a home whilst personal and/or family difficulties could be resolved. Usually after a period of some two years tenants moved into a permanent home.

or:-

- enable people to obtain suitable permanent housing in their own neighbourhood, for example Waterloo Crescent/Waterloo Road.

As we shall see later, Family First's ability to be innovative has been hindered by imposed regulation. The best environment for innovation in housing, in order to challenge prejudice and to meet people's needs, is to work flexibly and close to the grass roots. There was a conviction in Family First that it could (a) achieve successful innovative housing and social action locally, and (b) trigger wider interest and change, to enable other schemes to develop in ways appropriate to their own localities.

This happened very quickly. From the start, Family First's approach to housing young lone mothers attracted interest, including articles in the major national Press.

It was asked to advise Government departments, including the Home Office; local authorities, and voluntary bodies. Family First offered advisory support for new housing and self-help projects in many parts of the UK and overseas (including the USA, Trinidad and Australia).

An early UK scheme to take up Family First's ideas was the Sheffield Mother and Child Housing Association (SMACHA). In 1968, I addressed a large audience in Sheffield Town Hall to inaugurate the launch of SMACHA's neighbourhood housing project for seven mothers.

The Lord Mayor of Sheffield, Alderman Mrs Patience Sheard, said: ***"The ironical thing about England and most of the western world is that we all agree society has a responsibility to the abandoned, deserted and neglected child and are willing to spend untold amounts of money on these children. But we have totally neglected unmarried mothers and deserted wives who would be only too happy looking after their own child provided a certain amount of money was available."*** Sheffield Evening Telegraph (1968).

As mentioned in the previous chapter, Family First quickly developed a range of flexible services. To begin with, Family First's staff was myself as Director and a part-time assistant, Muriel Sutherland, previously a legal secretary. She was to stay with Family First for nine years, most of them as Manager of its Personal Services Department responsible by 1974 for dealing with four or five new serious requests for help each day and maintaining links with many families and individuals. Social workers from statutory departments in the city would often phone her for advice. She and I, and very soon a team of able volunteers, managed what – looking back – seems an amazing amount of work. We interviewed, trained and welcomed every volunteer who made a serious offer of help. And there were many.

The first full-time paid member of staff was an initially untrained and exceptionally talented teenager who also needed a home. Valerie Hands (later Springthorpe) became THE General Assistant. She lived with my family for some months from 1967. She lived an adventurous, creative life (in recent years in Scotland), and sadly died in 2005. Next was Susan French, Housing Manager, who joined in 1970.

Within a year, some young people Family First had helped became active volunteers themselves. When Family First advertised in the *Nottingham Evening Post* for financial support toward its project in Alexandra Park, many modest anonymous donations arrived. I wondered if some of these were from people with experience of being a lone parent.

When Family First started, the stigma of being a young lone mother often caused her to be thrown out of home and/or disowned. Not only was Family First criticised for housing young single parents, but also for housing families from all ethnic backgrounds. At that time, it was still common to see landlords' notices stating: "No Irish, No Blacks" and often: "No Children."

"It is a pity that these young people [single mothers] should be favoured in their folly. Why should they not be made to realise their misdeeds and work out their own salvation?" Signed VIRTUE [the capital letters were the letter-writer's!], *Nottingham Evening Post* March 1966.

The harshest critics were often people with little reason to feel superior. One person would sometimes shout abuse (of a racial variety) beneath my bedroom window in the middle of the night. Some years later, she and her husband turned to Family First for help for their daughter and it was offered.

Early housing solutions

Family First could not provide a substantial base of housing for the first couple of years, so it set out to find homes in different ways. Considering the extent of prejudice at that time, it was phenomenal how soon many people stood up to be counted and got involved. Writing this book has caused me to reflect why so many diverse volunteers emerged, for example, to help to provide, improve and find accommodation. The answer has something to do with people feeling (a) that they could actually make a difference, (b) that there were no status or other barriers, (c) that there were safeguards but no bureaucracy, and (d) that direct contact with people 'in need' quickly brought an earthy realisation that 'they' and 'us' are indistinguishable.

Here are a few examples of Family First's early housing solutions:-

*A family in Bramcote offered a room to a homeless pregnant woman or a mother with baby until a longer-term solution was found. Family First was available for support to both the host family and any young woman staying with it. Several did, sometimes for a week or two: one for many months.

*I walked around streets to spot empty properties in reasonable condition and then found out who owned them. If, for example, an empty house belonged to an elderly person permanently in a residential home, usually that person was happy for Family First to pay regular rent, and to take care of the house in return for sub-letting it on a fair basis to a homeless family. A contract would be drawn up. Such a house would need cleaning and decorating. One of Family First's supporting groups (e.g. women's groups, church groups, professional groups, trade union groups . . .) would 'adopt' a house, take responsibility for making it welcoming and safe, and manage it. Different people within the group would undertake the landlord role, such as collecting rent, and any befriending role. The latter was an optional choice for any tenant. Some long-lasting equal relationships evolved.

*If a lone mother wished to work, a suitable job with accommodation might be found. Again, a contract would be drawn up, safeguarding both parties. In the 1960s, this could be a preferred option. Times were very different, and people from close-knit neighbourhoods did not always wish to be as independent as might now be the case. Care was taken to sift out genuine offers of job/accommodation from the occasional dubious ones.

*In 1968, students of Nottingham University raised funds from their Carnival to enable Family First to purchase a house for use by a deserted mother and her five children. They had been 'in care' due to accommodation problems.

*"***I have read the advertisement inserted by Ron Stewart offering £30 towards buying a home for the Family First Trust. To my knowledge, no person in real need is refused help by Family First and such an association needs all the help – financial or otherwise – that people can offer.***" K Austen's letter in the ***Nottingham Evening Post*** (1969). The writer was a neighbour of Family First's and a volunteer on many occasions. Ron Stewart, a Deputy Charge Nurse, also a volunteer who lived in Mapperley, offered £30 if 99 other people did the same and thus raised the deposit on a house. It happened.

*Accommodation was found to fit individual needs. For example, for a couple of years while a young mother completed her nursing training involving shift work, she lived with a family that Family First found by advertising and then vetting. Family and young mum respected each other's privacy. When at work, her baby was cared for alongside the children of the host family. The baby grew up to be loved by grandparents who at first had pressed for adoption. Adoption did sometimes happen after a young mother considered what was best in her particular situation. Family First would continue support if requested.

*Mrs Khym See wrote (2003): "***I was destitute in 1969 with a two-and-a-half-year old child. I contacted Family First and was put into a flat over the Family First shop at 165, Carlton Road [a property Family First rented]. We had a beautiful large room, big fireplace and shared kitchen and bathroom with Theresa and her 18-month-old son. I still have my rent book. The accommodation was warm, cosy, safe and I loved it, and I can now say thank you. We were very broke but very happy. Our rooms were snug and welcoming. I helped in the shop sometimes ... Life has certainly been an adventure for me since 1933 but I only dwell on the good things, like Family First . . . I often see the FF van go past my house and I thank God it existed when I needed it. I am very proud to tell people I was a Family First tenant.***"

*Theresa wrote (2005): "***I was about to give my son up for adoption (1969) because we were homeless and hungry. I contacted several organisations to no avail. I went to a local Police Station and they sent me to Social Services, who gave me the name of Family First. I remember walking into The Croft and meeting Ruth. There was something about that place that made me feel safe. I knew we would be all right. Family First was like a big family, happy and sad at times, but always welcoming. The concept of The Croft was very new and there were people who thought it wouldn't work. Well, Family First is still here! My father never spoke to me for 20 years. Mom had to do what he said . . .***

"***The thing I remember about Family First is they were always there to help you, to teach you to cope whilst letting you live your life. Some of the mothers were very young. I was 22 . . . I went to live over the shop at 165, Carlton Road for about two years. It was clean and comfortable, my son went to the local nursery . . .***"

Khym and Theresa became friends and moved into a Council flat together. "***We were able to furnish it from the Family First warehouse with the help of a grant.***" Both women now have their own homes and are still friends. Khym's son is married and Theresa, who runs her own catering business, has three sons and is a grandmother.

Below are examples of housing that Family First has provided and provides today.

Mayholme/The Croft

Family First's first owned housing project at Mayholme/The Croft, Alexandra Park, Nottingham, was the outcome to the answers from young lone mothers to this question: "***How might it be possible to create a secure housing environment that enabled young lone parents to feel that life was***

positive; that allowed them to make sound choices about their future, and which offered them opportunity to feel involved on equal but not special terms?" Their answers, expressed differently, amounted to wanting responsibility for their baby in a safe housing environment with a few other mums in a similar situation nearby, and an older person to turn to for advice and support when needed. Their hope sounded so straightforward and simple but, for many, unobtainable prior to Family First.

Funding for Mayholme/The Croft was secured from major trusts including the Gulbenkian Foundation. The property was converted into bright modern bed-sits for eight young women, pregnant or with babies; Family First's administrative office; a large community room; a general purpose room; a large shared kitchen in addition to kitchen facilities in tenants' rooms, and a maisonette where my family lived. Mayholme/The Croft opened officially early in 1967. On the land, when funds allowed, would be built a small office extension, 14 flats for mixed use and a family centre including a 30-place day nursery.

The project owed a lot to the Gulbenkian Foundation. Deputy Director Richard Mills wrote 10 years after Family First started (1975): ***"Occasionally a new application [for grant] makes an instant appeal to both heart and mind. This was one of them . . . As the first successful embodiment of contemporary ideas of the one-parent family's needs and how they should be met, your organisation points the way forward, not just for Nottingham, but the country as a whole . . . The comfortable, bright homelike atmosphere of The Croft – the very antithesis of the old institutional character of such places in the past – epitomised Family First's non-judgemental, accepting and caring attitude to those whom it sought to help towards an independent, full life."***

When this innovative project was at the planning stage, I was pressurised by 'experts' to create virtually a closed community with its own labour suite and professional staff. But the founding idea was for Family First to be part of the wider community and for tenants to access all normal services. If a tenant had a social worker or probation officer, for example, it was better for them to come to The Croft, as did doctors, midwives, health visitors and so on. In this way The Croft was part of an open community and its standards were visible.

The project was neither called a hostel nor run like one. I was not paid as the responsible resident person. It was important at that time to break from the tradition of paid warden. Not being paid for this responsibility or, in the first few years, as Director of Family First allowed me freedom to be with my three children in school holidays. I boosted family income when necessary by, for example, part-time teaching of newly immigrant young teenagers and also apprentice joiners on day release. For many of the years 1965-1976, my then husband was away all weekdays and, for the last two-and-a-half years, I was myself a lone breadwinner parent. I valued the sense of community that Family First offered.

A former volunteer, Linda Hill, wrote (2005) about a recollection that illustrated how the project was designed in all details not to be institutional: ***"I can well remember you coming to speak to the Soroptimist International of Nottingham Trent Valley in 1965 at the Elite Buildings about your plans for the project. I became involved in making curtains for some of the rooms at The Croft. You had this (fantastic to me at the time!) idea of doubling up the fabric, so that it looked good from the inside and out, and was quite a challenge to spread correctly for stitching! However, the effect was very satisfactory. Later I made the curtains for the flat above the Family First shop in Mapperley."***

Tenants at Mayholme/The Croft were aged between 15 to early 20s: a few were older. During my years as resident family, 134 young mothers lived there. I am still in touch with some of them and hear about others through mutual friends. One of the innovations was allowing a tenant's boyfriend (often her baby's father) to visit: after midday and before 10.30 p.m. Traditional mother and baby homes kept fathers out.

Fathers sometimes took considerable responsibility for their babies. Some parents worked towards a future together. Relationships, hastily undertaken, were usually worked out with maturity and thought for the baby. No two situations were the same. A few mothers did not know who their baby's father was. Whatever the circumstance of its conception, each new baby deserves the best chance possible in life.

There had to be a few house rules. Some mothers were on probation or under other statutory restrictions. For fire safety, there was need to know who was in the house at night. Coming-in time was 10.30 p.m. except for special occasions and agreed at least 24 hours in advance. Overnight stays away had to be agreed and an address given in advance: having a baby meant serious responsibility. Any hostility to such negotiations soon melted because of the shared sense of looking out for each other. Sometimes two mothers who became friends shared a flat when they left. Friendships between tenants still exist all these years on.

In summer 1976, tenants and staff welcomed Kathy and Peter Clay as the new voluntary resident family. Some years earlier, Kathy Clay was a Family First tenant. She was a long-standing active volunteer contributing to Family First in general and life at The Croft Family Centre in particular. With three children – plus Kathy's nephew after her sister's death – Kathy and Peter Clay creatively sustained and developed life in Mayholme/The Croft. Peter continued working outside but helped in the evenings and at weekends. When Peter's work moved, the Clay family moved to Wales.

From 1980 to 1992, Maggie and Steve Elford were the voluntary resident family with their three young children. A fourth was born whilst there. I met Maggie and Steve Elford in Nottingham in 2004. They said they enjoyed their time at Mayholme/The Croft and learned a lot that has been useful since. Steve continued his outside job with BT. Maggie also did some childminding and still does.

As the 1980s advanced, ideas were changing. Occasionally tenants resented the fact that boyfriends could not stay overnight if they wished. Family First took the view that if a couple wanted to be together, they should accept responsibility for that decision and did not need Mayholme/The Croft. It was not acceptable for a boyfriend to latch on to a young mother and expect residency. Usually, a young mother quickly discovered if a boyfriend was helpful or parasitical. Better she discovered this whilst in a secure environment. She could ask that a 'boyfriend' should not visit.

From listening to Maggie and Steve, it was clear that by the late 1980s the needs of young mothers to gain knowledge and confidence remained constant. Maggie remembered special times: for example, when a young mother without family support needed her to be there during the early stages of labour.

Towards the end of Maggie and Steve's time at Mayholme/The Croft, they said the Community Room became used ***"more and more for meetings of the Housing Committee people"*** and less by tenants. At that time, Family First's Housing Sub-Committee also dominated the Management Committee. This is clearly evident from the archives. Some Committee members keen to foster neighbourhood involvement had moved away or retired. And the 'overt' business culture, prevalent nationally – and politically endorsed at that time – was also affecting Family First. These matters are mentioned elsewhere. Maggie and Steve Elford said a lot changed in Family First after Angus Walker left (1988). It began to get ***"a bit corporate".***

Another resident family briefly followed Maggie and Steve Elford before Family First's then Director Graham Wright ended the voluntary resident family system in Family First properties (see Resident families section below).

In 1994, the large Community Room, leading off the lobby inside The Croft front door, was divided into offices and offices took over some of the first floor. The accommodation for young mothers moved across into Mayholme, including space formerly used by resident families. In accordance with Housing Corporation categories, Mayholme was now to be a 'hostel' and it became called one in everyday conversation. With the demise of the voluntary resident family, paid support staff were recruited. A room was available in Mayholme for an office and, later, for overnight shifts.

There were then seven tenants (previously the number varied from six to 10). The age range for a short while, in 1995, was limited to16 to18. Coincidentally, there was nobody in a supporting role 24/7 due to lack of funding. This did not work and, perhaps predictably, led to problems with a minority of boyfriends, e.g. making noise in the neighbourhood in the evenings. Some neighbourhood goodwill was lost at this time. The issues were addressed and proper staffing arranged, including a security person at night for the whole site.

For more than 25 years before it was divided into offices, including almost a decade before The Croft Family Centre was opened, all manner of events took place in The Croft Community Room. This spacious room allowed the informal (always voluntary) mixing of young mothers at Mayholme/The Croft with neighbours, other Family First tenants, volunteers, staff, students and others. Such events included ceilidhs, birthday parties, occasional wedding receptions, celebratory meals, and mums and toddlers' groups. Then there were evening classes organised at the request of or by tenants. Most importantly, it was space where people could hang out together to chat. There was no TV. Tenants could have TVs in their rooms if they wished.

Tenants were kept in the picture about anything special being planned. For example, as founder Vice-Chair of Radio Nottingham, I threw a party when it was one year old and the young tenants joined in the all-age gathering. When the adjoining Family Centre and 14 flats on the site were built and opened in 1974/75, the role of The Croft Community Room became even more important.

From the mid-1990s, support workers were available round-the-clock. By 2004 this was funded via the Government's new Supporting People programme. But by 2005 this funding was already curtailed, necessitating staff cuts. One problem in the current statutory social policy/funding culture is that 'support' and 'care' are separately funded. When, for instance, a statutory agency wishes to place a young mother at Mayholme/The Croft, it may not be willing/able to fund the costs of the 'care' requested.

Support is supposed to encourage independence and care is hands-on help. In the real world it is unworkable to attach vetoes to any overlap of these functions. To illustrate this point: when I was resident person at Mayholme/The Croft, a scared young mother became physically ill. She suffered serious abuse in childhood and wanted very much to be a good mother and to learn new skills. When her baby cried and she was too weak to cope on her own, she feared that he would be taken 'into care'. Some practical help was the natural solution offered by a capable neighbour or myself in the presence of the mother.

Over the years, the content of rent has changed. One recent change was described thus by a staff member: ***"Any cost for support was taken out of Housing Benefit, and went into the Government's Supporting People programme."*** This programme makes a variable grant payment to Family First for Mayholme/The Croft residents. Staff have to treat 'care' and 'support' as different. If you are paid through a Government 'support' programme, you may not bath or feed a baby (even in emergency) because that is 'care' and funded from a different source. And, to compound the situation, should you mix your roles, or involve a capable volunteer, 'risk' assessment issues come into view!

"When someone is vulnerable, the first priority is to make sure they are OK. Switching off and on what is 'care' can become a business and not a practical issue. That's wrong." Staff member (2003).

"Whatever you would like to do because it is needed, you have the [official] form, and you have to jiggle round whatever is needed into 'their' categories. If you simply put what is needed, it gets thrown out. It doesn't get a look-in." A senior staff member on the matter of funding (2003).

Today's society is superficially very different from that of the 1960s and 1970s. Though few families would now reject a single daughter if she became pregnant, she may have to move out because of lack of space. Keeping a baby and abortion are more prevalent. Then, as now, teenage mothers may have been raised 'in care' or experienced very dysfunctional homes. But their basic needs are still to be in safe accommodation, to be able to turn to someone for advice, to allow their competence and confidence to develop and to tackle any underlying problems. These may include drug use, need to complete basic education, and to accept responsibility for decisions including relationship with a boyfriend. There are not as many deserted young wives today because marriage is not as prevalent among the young.

Prejudice thrust at young mothers can still be very harsh. But whereas in the 1960s society could be punitive toward young 'unmarried' or 'unsupported' mothers, now it can be punitive towards 'teenage' mothers. 'Facts' about young mothers are often confused, for example, with misleading tabloid newspaper headlines about young girls getting pregnant in order to obtain Council flats quickly, or an atypical sensational story about a particular pregnant teenager. The fact that even 18 can now be regarded – in principle – as 'too young' would have surprised previous generations. This is a wide issue. Accurate statistics are available from www.oneparentfamilies.org.uk.

If you have an operation in a Nottingham hospital, you may be well cared for by a former young Family First tenant. If you have a child in school, he or she may be taught by a former teenage tenant. Many former young lone tenants are loving grandparents. Children born to Mayhome/The Croft young mothers have mostly taken very positive paths in life. Even looked at in cold economics they have already made a huge positive contribution to society.

What next at Mayholme/The Croft?

Over the past four decades, Family First has had as much, or more, practical experience as any agency in the UK of working with young lone mothers to enable them to become independent, capable parents. The Project Manager at Mayholme/The Croft is Marketa McNally (2005). The project is thriving but its fabric needs renewing.

To celebrate its 40th anniversary, Family First started raising funds in order that Mayholme/The Croft can EITHER be thoroughly rehabilitated OR replaced. What is needed?

(1) Funding of £400,000+. A significant part of this has been raised. Those helping the 40th Anniversary Appeal included young mothers currently living at Mayholme/The Croft.

(2) A regulatory environment that allows and does not stifle the degree of innovation needed. Bold and imaginative vision is needed for the future as it was 40 years ago. By the late 1970s, we believed society was gradually becoming more equal. Today it is becoming rapidly more divided. Never has there been more need for local bold but cost-effective innovation.

I received the following from Mayholme young mothers aged between ages 16 and 21 in 2005. Their stories are not essentially different from those of many of the young lone mothers who came to The Croft in the 1960s:-

*"***I was 15 when I had my baby. When I was pregnant I didn't want to keep my baby so I was going to put her up for adoption. When I had my baby girl, I didn't give her up because all my family was behind me all the way and looked after me . . . In the end I had a Home Tutor and did my GCSEs . . . People can think what they like about young mums but they will never know until they are in our shoes.***"* L.

*"***I was 18 when I had my daughter and 19 when I had my son. I moved to Mayholme to see if I could cope with my son. I find it easy to cope with him. I decided to keep my kids to give them a chance in life. My daughter still lives with her grandparents but I see her every day. Her dad takes drugs and drinks a lot. I do not intend to be with him.***"* K.

*"***I was 17 when I fell pregnant. I was on the depo injection but they say no contraceptive is 100%. Everyone's experience is different. I thought my partner would be OK as he had a little girl from a previous relationship, but he wasn't and we split up. I had a lot of support from my family . . . as much as I love her I wish I had waited***

a few years. It's not like having a doll. You can't just put them away when you've had enough of them. They need 24-hour care, feeding, playing, loving. Sometimes, I'm up at 5.30ish playing, teaching her to grow. Babies are so special. If it wasn't for all the support I've had, then it would have been harder. " S.

"I went to the hospital with my Nanna and did a test. When I found out, I rang J and he was pleased. I was scared to tell my family so my Nanna told them. My mum thinks me and J won't cope with a baby on our own. I think we will. I will be 17 when my baby's born. We've both had experience with children so I don't think it will be that hard. No-one pressurised me about having an abortion. I don't agree with abortions." S.

Other early years properties

Although the Local Authority refused (1968) a loan to build 14 flats on land at The Croft, Family First purchased properties through other loans and fund-raising. It struggled to gain planning permission to purchase houses in 'mixed' areas: the City Council wanted it to purchase them in the most 'difficult' ones. Properties bought were in Mapperley, Forest Fields and the Forest side of Radford and Hyson Green, i.e. in mixed areas with amenities nearby including shops and bus routes. It created a geographical focus for Family First that was desirable for tenants and for local administration. Tenants could use The Croft Community Room and, from 1975, the newly built Croft Family Centre: also from 1980 the Crescent Community Centre on Waterloo Road.

I received a letter (2001) from a former Family First tenant [flat in Mapperley]. M said she was probably quite 'difficult' when a tenant because of what had happened to her. She wanted to say what – many years ago – she never managed to say: thank you. She is now a teacher. It is always good to know that people who were deep in problems have come through.

Late 1960s/early 1970s

Purchases varied from single family occupancy houses to large structurally sound Victorian houses which needed rehabilitating and modernising. They were divided into three or four self-contained housing units. The modernisation was thorough and lasted at least 20 years before some more upgrading was needed. Usually one unit would be for a single person, two for one-parent families and one for a voluntary resident family who itself needed accommodation.

Resident families

From 1967 to the early 1990s, there were voluntary resident families in Family First properties with four or more housing units. They met regularly for support and to share experiences. They had fewer responsibilities than the resident family at Mayholme/The Croft. They paid a slightly reduced rent in return for collecting rents weekly, reporting maintenance needed, keeping gardens/yards tidy, and acting as 'good neighbours' to Family First tenants and 'next door' people. They welcomed new tenants and helped those leaving.

When visiting from Perth, Australia, a few years ago, Penny and David Hilditch recalled their years as resident family in a four-flat house in Hyson Green. They said they learned much of value to their future life. On one occasion, a distressed tenant knocked on their door and reported: ***"M [another tenant] has turned into a monster!"*** The 'monster' was swollen all over and had suffered an acute allergic reaction after a medical injection. Penny and David drove her to hospital and were told she might have died without prompt treatment. With patience and talking, David on one occasion disarmed the threatening ex-husband of a tenant. He was holding a large knife. Penny and David remember especially an elderly eccentric woman two doors away who thought Family First was wonderful because they occasionally helped her with shopping.

The resident family system was ended in the early 1990s. I am told that the then Director, Graham Wright, agreed to this because of the Housing Corporation's difficulty in accepting the practice.

Nottingham's Family First 1965-2005 ISBN 09550948 01

Each tenant faced his or her own challenge. For example, a young man was in a psychiatric hospital longer than necessary because his parents rejected him, following a motor accident in which he sustained head injuries. He became a Family First volunteer whilst, at first, still living in hospital. Then he became independently housed in a Family First single-person flat. Later he accomplished his wishes: to marry, to do useful work in the community and to have his own home. Living a skilful, contented life, he became a good neighbour to many people.

In 1970/71, Family First asked six social workers to keep brief summaries of single young women's histories that might offer clues to what was needed with regard to housing/back-up support. Fifteen brief histories of unnamed 15 to 24-year-olds, who were homeless or on the edge of homelessness, were offered as 'samples'. Here is one of them. It is, by no means, the most complicated.

"Aged 17. Two brothers and one sister. Lived with parents until she went to a probation hostel at 16. No exams at school and no idea of what she wanted for a career. Poor work record. Played truant a lot from school. Has been treated for VD. Very overweight. Tidy and dresses well. Would like to live by herself. Has poor relationship with parents and feels they have let her down. No boyfriend. Not interested in money – will scrounge if necessary. Feels unsettled but unwilling to discuss future. Drinks a lot."

Once its neighbourhood scheme in Waterloo Crescent /Waterloo Road was completed, Family First used two adjoining linked properties as accommodation for young adults of both sexes (see below). Before that, from 1971 for some years, it had a property in Mapperley housing a resident family and six young women leaving statutory hostels at age 16. This was run in co-operation with the Probation Department.

Family First often received non-housing requests because it was an organisation that "***understood young people***". For example, a young woman wrote: ***"Could you possibly help me with making a friendship with someone in a similar situation. I am 20, unmarried with a little girl. I have no friends in Nottingham."*** Family First tried hard to meet such requests with care. Very often, now as then, young people know what they need in order to progress positively. They deserve to be heard. Underlying Family First's work is a determination to try to prevent social isolation, which triggers, now as in earlier decades, many problems including anti-social behaviour and depression.

As mentioned above, Family First purchased a house from funds raised by Nottingham University students (1968) at their annual Carnival. Students helped generously on several other occasions. The public were often generous. For example, Family First appealed for funds to enable it to purchase and renovate a house for one of the families arriving in the UK in 1972 after Idi Amin expelled all Ugandan Asians. A house in Forest Fields quickly housed a three-generation Ugandan Asian family. They established themselves and a few years later moved to London near another family member. They hoped future tenants would enjoy ***"the same opportunity"***. Housing Manager Phil Tetlow and I were invited to share their farewell feast.

In 1970, the Southwell Diocesan Board of Moral Welfare [now Southwell Diocesan Council for Family Care], whose staff referred clients to Family First, offered Family First its property in Mapperley. For many years, it was the traditionally run Diocesan hostel for single pregnant mothers and their babies. Family First converted it into self-contained flats. At this time, housing associations were expected to conform to Parker Morris standards. The Parker Morris Committee's 1961 report on public housing specified a generous space allocation per person in every housing unit.

Sometimes, a one-parent family accustomed to living close to other people found the 'legal' amount of space intimidating and Family First might arrange a shared tenancy to help tenants to feel safe. Family First was prepared to defend this action, believing people's genuine needs more important than a specified measurement: which does not mean that standards are irrelevant. Parker Morris standards were dropped in the 1980s.

In 1970, a property on Mapperley 'Top' was purchased as Family First's first owned shop with a flat above. In 1972, Family First purchased another shop, plus flat, at 116, Leslie Road, in Forest Fields: all local Family First tenants would pay their rent at the shop, which became a focus of neighbourhood friendship for many years, eventually closing on October 1st, 2004. In 1974, Family First purchased a shop at 95, Ilkeston Road with flat above (see Recycling chapter).

Occasionally, a Family First tenant caused some nuisance: any complaint was taken seriously. But there were more instances of prejudice about tenants. For example, a near neighbour of a Family First house in Mapperley complained that its tenants held a noisy party late into the night. Without first notifying Family First, a leading city councillor circulated all neighbours for their views about Family First. Some were angry at his approach and contacted me. The alleged noise had indeed happened, but in an owner-occupied house next to the Family First one! I met the councillor concerned and told him. He said: ***"Oh that's all right then if they own their house."*** I strongly disagreed: either people were making a nuisance or they were not!

By 1972, Family First was advancing its plans to build 14 flats and a Family Centre in the grounds of The Croft. It was also exploring the possibility of a neighbourhood rehabilitation scheme (see below).

A house in Premier Road, Nottingham, was donated (1974) by Mr and Mrs H E Gunton. After nearly a decade, Family First had become a trusted local organisation and many people were incredibly generous. Within Family First, there is a sizeable accumulation of financial community capital that should remain a local resource for the future.

The early rehabilitated properties had modern kitchens, with space for a fridge and, usually, a washing machine. In the 1960s, the level of income of tenants on benefit or in low-paid jobs often meant a choice in cold weather between food or heat. They could not afford to run central heating. They needed heating sources that were easily controlled. Family First initially modernised homes using new gas fires in sitting rooms and on/off electric heating in other rooms. The first satisfactory heating/hot water systems were slimline storage heaters providing constant warmth and a 210 cylinder supplying hot water at affordable rates through 'Economy 7' tariff. Tenant response confirmed this was a favoured heating/hot water system. There was one bill, new card meters to help with family budgeting and ample supply of hot water. In 1989, the Property Services Manager, Denis Kelleher, reported that standard electric meters had been or would also be changed for 'Economy 7' meters in Family First hostels, shops, the day nursery, and all other projects. Other changes were instigated to save energy and costs.

846, Woodborough Road

Purchased in 1974, this defective house in Mapperley was pulled down. Family First built a small infill block of eight one-bedroom flats for local elderly people. It already owned the next door shop property, 848, Woodborough Road.

The demolition of 846, Woodborough Road was the largest project so far undertaken, under skilled supervision, by trainees and by offenders doing community work in place of a custodial sentence. The property was popular with elderly tenants due to nearness to a comprehensive shopping complex and a direct bus route into Nottingham city centre.

The back of the house provided a pleasant large garden and garage/store, used for some years by Family First's Furniture Service, with entrance on to a side street. Some of this land was sold to a developer in 2005 to assist housing finances.

Lorna Court and Mary Court at The Croft

These two-storey courts with 14 flats were planned at Family First's inception and became possible following a donation of £54,000 from Lorna Mary Wilkinson (see Bequests). One was tenanted in 1974: the other in 1975.

At the same time, a self-contained first-floor flat was added to the rear of The Croft

Nottingham's Family First 1965-2005 ISBN 09550948 01

on a flat roof. A small office extension at the front was built much earlier. In summer 1975, the new-build Croft Family Centre opened and all building on this pleasant site was then complete.

The new flats were for a mix of one-parent families and other tenants. They included a young physically disabled woman whose parents had been murdered and a woman aged over 90 who needed an easy to manage home. She wished to be among younger people. The benefit was mutual. Some families needed considerable back-up in order to become fully independent, including a pregnant woman who had spent years unnecessarily in a psychiatric hospital. She was determined to keep her child and had to prove her competence to social workers. She did.

The homes in Lorna Court and Mary Court have been in continuous full use for over thirty years so far.

Waterloo Crescent/Waterloo Road neighbourhood scheme

Family First wished to undertake a neighbourhood rehabilitation scheme and proposed doing this at Waterloo Crescent and Waterloo Road, a potentially beautiful 19th century crescent around a grassy area with mature trees and near the Forest recreation ground. ***"By the early 1970s, it [the area] had become an embarrassment to the City Council to which houses reverted as leases expired, since the houses were large, and dilapidated, but being part of a Conservation Area couldn't be demolished.***[1]***"***

This idea was rejected by the City Council in 1972. The City Estates Surveyor said: ***"The present feeling of the Estates Committee who own and control these properties is that they should be converted by and remain under the control of the Corporation."***

However, Family First was encouraged to look for another neighbourhood of properties. After a second area was rejected, it made a detailed feasibility study of 107 houses on Cromwell Street and one side of Portland Road. Many owners/occupiers in an active residents and tenants' association wanted to prevent their homes being demolished as part of the Nottingham Raleigh Street Clearance Area. More than two-thirds of the households, 68.54%, wished to stay in the area. The Council's proposals allowed only for a 26% population replacement.

In the Family First scheme, only seven houses needed to be demolished. Just before Family First was registered with the Housing Corporation in 1975, it and the Department of the Environment were hopeful for this scheme subject to Nottingham City Council's approval. However, the City Council refused, but – using the detail of the feasibility study – the Raleigh Street Residents and Tenants' Association won an appeal that saved some of their homes.

The Cromwell Street project proposed by Family First was a good scheme. Many of the improved properties would have remained single family residences with a mix of flat sizes in the others. The area, with a large core of committed local tenants and residents, lent itself to improvement, including adding a playground and community building on a very human scale.

While turning down the Cromwell Street plan, the City Council offered Family First a fourth option. It was Waterloo Crescent/Waterloo Road!

Nottingham architect Andrew James said: ***"By the time we got on site [at Waterloo Crescent in January 1977] almost every scrap of metal had disappeared including lead from flat roofs, all internal pipe-work – even the cast iron sash window weights. Windows were broken, sashes smashed, floorboards torn up and fires started. (One house was burnt through from cellar to roof.) The cost of delay in the deterioration of vacant houses is difficult to assess, but it is certainly substantial and unnecessary.***[2]***"***

Bridget Harry (nee Farrand) was one of three volunteers who interviewed people in the Cromwell Street area in the spring/summer 1974. She told me (2005): ***"It was my experience as a volunteer that encouraged me to work in the voluntary***

[1] *Waterloo Crescent: Architectural and technical aspects of large-scale rehabilitation* by Andrew James in *Architecture East Midlands*. March/April 1977

[2] Ibid

***housing sector. After a year at Hull University (completing a Diploma in Social Administration), I returned to Family First to work full time as a housing assistant for three years. After another year away at university (Bristol), I gained my social work qualification and returned to Family First.*"** She worked for Family First until 1990 when she was Housing Adviser.

Bridget Harry added: ***"I enjoyed changing the way that the housing service was delivered in the 1980s. The important aspect of this transition for me was not to lose sight of what it was good at, i.e. as a specialist housing provider for single parents and young single homeless people and a provider of permanent housing for people with local connections in the Waterloo Crescent area of Nottingham.***

"The main reason why I left (1990) was because the aims of FF were changing. In my view it wanted to compete with the larger housing associations whereas it should have remained a 'small' (I think the definition was then under 250 housing units) and specialist organisation."

When I left Family First as Director in 1976, it had 82 housing units of varying sizes. The Waterloo Crescent/Waterloo Road neighbourhood scheme was ready to 'take off'. The rehabilitation work was achieved around some long-term sitting tenants, many of them stalwart elderly women who wished to stay. They had lived there for a long time, including a decade of local decay. They were surrounded by empty, vandalised properties. Some of their flats were old-fashioned and not always self-contained. Family First went to huge lengths to respect their wishes. It believed that wherever caring people existed in a neighbourhood, they should be regarded as its prime asset, not an impediment to progress. Tenants in 2005 were of varying ages, size of households and diverse backgrounds.

The first phase of 12 houses was completed in 1978. Although identical in appearance from the front, the houses showed 19th century speculative builders' ingenuity in varied plan forms. This created rehabilitation opportunities for a mixture of dwelling size and plan types. The mix was 20% self-contained bed-sitters (in hostels), 40% one-bedroom flat/maisonettes, 30% two-bedroom flat/maisonettes, and 10% three-bedroom flat/maisonettes. Funding and planning consent were not available for making larger units. In order to create some neighbourhood focus, Family First opened the Crescent Community Centre at 34, Waterloo Road.

Family First purchased other properties in the Waterloo Crescent/Waterloo Road neighbourhood, including (1982) Millers House, a complex of three terrace houses on nearby Forest Road.

Waterloo Crescent and Waterloo Road hostels

Two modern hostels were created: at 91-93, Waterloo Crescent and 30-32, Waterloo Road. Between 1978 and 2005, these hostels housed at least 3,000 people, including occupants of a follow-on house in Mapperley. For many, life improved as a result. For a significant number, it improved beyond their dreams. The hostels were practical projects for people who, for too long, had been largely overlooked. Over the years, these two hostels also involved trainees doing placements toward their certificate (CQSW) to qualify as social workers and other helpers (including an ex-hostel tenant on a Youth Training Programme).

91-93, Waterloo Crescent

The hostel at 91-93, Waterloo Crescent was for homeless men. Managed by the then recently formed Macedon Trust from 1978, the hostel provided a sense of security and community for a group more used to overnight refuges or sleeping rough. The building included a workshop. More than a decade later, it ran into temporary difficulties due to a phase of poor administration. Former Family First Director Angus Walker then running his own business, was asked to sort out the management and financial structures. The hostel continued with a new manager until, in 1993, it was refurbished and opened by Councillor Sylvia Parsons as a 12-bedroom hostel managed by Family First for young single people (an extension to its work at 30-32, Waterloo Road).

From 1999 for a few years, Nottingham Help the Homeless Association managed 91-93, Waterloo Crescent for single homeless people affected by mental health issues or other problems. Then, the property became managed by Framework [the merger association of Nottingham Help the Homeless and the Macedon Trust]. Framework houses and supports homeless people, and offers care and support to residents who also have issues such as substance abuse and offending behaviour, whilst some have mild learning difficulties.

Framework purchased the property from Family First (2005) under the right-to-buy clause in their tenancy agreement. So this hostel has a continuing history of housing and supporting people at a very difficult time in their lives.

30-32, Waterloo Road

This hostel, across the tree-lined grassy area from 91-93, Waterloo Crescent, dared to challenge concepts of how to support young people, especially those who grew up 'in care' and who – in their mid-teens – were often ill-equipped for independent living. Growing up 'in care' could be, and still can be, very difficult.

This hostel owed much to its resident family from 1981, Pat and Richard Morfett. For the first two years, they were the only staff. Their practical vision reinforced Family First's determination not to be hemmed in by prejudice or to accept that young people with problems were intrinsically problem people. Pat and Richard Morfett had four children: the fourth was born during their stay as resident family. In 1986, Richard became first Director of the Nottingham Hostels Liaison Group. When Richard and Pat Morfett moved out as resident family in 1986, Pat became Family First's project leader for Mayholme/The Croft; 30-32, Waterloo Road; 91-93, Waterloo Crescent; for a time 101, Waterloo Crescent, and a move-on house for six residents about half-a-mile from Waterloo Crescent.

Pat Morfett (2005) said her involvement with Family First started in 1977 when she volunteered for the Parents Anonymous phoneline, a project set up by Family First's community worker, Maria Dabrowska, and Dr Sandra Buck, a volunteer in Family First's day nursery and a neighbour of Mayhome/The Croft as well as a member of Family First's Management Committee for some years. The plan for 30-32, Waterlooo Road was to develop a supported housing project for young people leaving statutory care, using Mayholme /The Croft as a model.

The hostel had an open door policy. Anticipating that residents would stay at least six months, there was time to build up relationships. Residents could begin to sort out their 'baggage'.

After the hostel opened, Pat Morfett said (2005) referrals came thick and fast from staff of children's homes looking for supported housing options for 15 and 16-year-olds.*"We gradually built up good relationships with some social workers. During the early 1980s, we ran a number of 'leaving care' groups [from the next door Crescent Community Centre] with a social worker and Social Services funding. Dr Sandra Buck supported the groups giving contraceptive advice and leading discussions on responsibilities and relationships.*

"One group chose to focus on their relationships with their carers. Some young people could not remember all their foster placements or all the different Local Authority placements. There were some outstanding carers and social workers that young people spoke about with affection but there were also stories of abuse . . . The groups gave the young people the confidence to speak out . . . I saw a dreadfully destructive resignation in virtually all of these young women.

"I remember one who had been in care all her life. She had been taken into care when a few weeks old: from healthy to struggling-to-survive in just a few weeks. She spent her life in foster care and residential placements and not really understanding why. In her early teens she told her social workers that she had been sexually abused by her foster father. She was later returned to that family. As part of the leaving care preparation, she was allowed to see her case files and, for the first time, she understood why she had been taken into care in the first place.

She was one of the exceptions in that she was very angry, channelling her anger to her social worker and her parents who by this time would not speak to her or let her into their house. She made 999 calls sending fire engines and ambulances to both houses. She sent excrement and soiled sanitary towels through the post to them. She did not deny what she was doing and asked me many times why she was being punished while the real criminals were unpunished. I had no answer to that and she became the responsibility of the mental health services."

The above story illustrates the close link, for many young people, between serious unresolved issues in their growing-up years and resultant mental health problems that were, and are, often due to having no voice that is heard when needed.

Often finding a basic living allowance for a young person involved negotiation with several statutory departments, sometimes a hospital as well, at a time when a young person needed a period of security in which to work through to a positive future.

Pat Morfett wrote to the DHSS (1988): ***"Would you please clarify the following situation as it affects a resident living in the Hostel and who has been given conflicting information. She is at present on a Youth Training Scheme [YTS] but would like to go to College to take a GCSE course. She was advised that she would not receive income support if she refused the YTS placement. However, after taking Welfare Rights advice, we believe that she could study full time (regulation 13) and receive income support."***

A letter to the Principal Assistant, Child Care, at Nottinghamshire County Council (1988) stated: ***"R moved to the follow-on house, referred by her social worker. We had several phone conversations with her culminating in the letter sent to her senior social worker (copy enclosed). R was subsequently told that she did not fit the criteria for a leaving care grant [£100] as she had left foster care and not residential care. Our understanding of the matter is that a young person is entitled to this grant regardless of whether it is foster or residential care."***

The Family First hostels on Waterloo Road and Waterloo Crescent were often struggling financially, including in 1989 when the Housing Corporation was monitoring Family First's progress over rent setting to meet new legislative demands. Cutting back on hostels would have been one way of easing Family First finances, but senior Family First staff claimed: ***"We are one of the few housing associations with expertise at running hostels and, whilst this does involve staff time [= cost], the provision of hostel accommodation is meeting a priority housing need."*** From minutes of an extraordinary meeting of the Family First Housing Sub-Committee.

The Minutes of a meeting (1991) of the Family First Management Committee with staff of 30-32, Waterloo Road record: ***"The effects of the October 1989 housing benefit changes are only now being fully appreciated. For the hostel staff, the changes have meant increased time spent helping residents with the complicated claim system. Clearly this means less time on other valuable tasks. For the residents, the changes have resulted in lower levels of benefit (once their claims are eventually processed) leading to increasing difficulty in budgeting. Often they have inadequate food and clothing and rent payments are missed. This eventually leads to eviction – a cycle of homelessness can be seen developing."***

A London trust made a timely substantial grant to assist funding this hostel. This was mainly due to national recognition of Family First's pioneer work in the neglected field of appropriate care for young people.

Reflecting on her time with Family First, Pat Morfett states (2005) how a combination of factors gradually adversely affected the: ***"positive times when we were able to focus on the young people and the relationships we had with them. So what changed and when? The Director, senior housing officers and key members of Family First Management Committee left [1988-1991]. Social Services reviewed and reorganised their policies so that we were working less with social workers and more with the City Council Homeless Section so that all our careful work to be part of a planning process for young people leaving care was redundant. And the changes in the benefits system were punitive, destructive and inflexible. I think that the***

most profound unintended consequences of these factors was that the focus shifted from the young people to survival: what we had to do to try and keep the project viable."

Family First's slightly late Thirtieth Anniversary Newsletter (spring 1996) said that Pat Morfett had left after 15 years, and added: ***"For the past ten years, Pat has been Project Leader and managed the Family First hostels through many changes including the move over to 91-93, Waterloo Crescent and an almost 50% increase in bed-spaces. Her commitment and her enthusiasm are greatly missed."***

In 1997, 30-32 ,Waterloo Road was awarded a 'Secured by Design' certificate after a comprehensive refit, including 15 bed-sits, in partnership with the Housing Corporation, Nottingham Health Authority and Nottinghamshire Police. During 1997 (when 91-93, Waterloo Crescent was also used for young people), the two hostels housed 98 young adults: 16 moved on to live in permanent accommodation. In 2001/02, 30-32, Waterloo Road became a project working toward Foyer accreditation and took the name The Waterloo Foyer. This was essentially an education development project 'with bed attached' for young people between the ages of 16 and 25. During 2003/04, 21 residents were assisted. The Foyer, funded through the new Government Supporting People grant, employed an education officer who planned activities for those living at the Foyer or those it was continuing to support.

"Since I started living at the Waterloo Foyer, I have joined a course called 'Entry into Employment' which is run by BESTCO [a training agency]. I attend the course each day from Monday to Thursday to study maths and English and they teach me spelling and reading, which I struggle with most. I like living in the Foyer because the staff are really helpful and they have guided me towards my career goals." Anna (2003).

"S joined the Foyer just over 12 months ago. It was discovered that she had learning difficulties which affected her communication and life skills . . . S had difficulties forming relationships with her peers and struggled to fulfil some of the issues identified in her support plan . . . The training she received within the Foyer helped S make real progress in developing her communication and life skills. S has had support to access another project that can further assist her goals. She is in regular contact with Foyer staff who visit her regularly to provide support." Foyer staff (2004).

The Foyer closed in March 2005 due to the withdrawal of Supporting People finance. The Board agreed to sell 30-32, Waterloo Road. The Board minute of June 8th 2005 reads: ***"It was noted that the [hostel] properties on Waterloo Road and Waterloo Crescent were a significant part of FF's history, and that, although it was good to see 91-93, Waterloo Crescent, passing to Framework, it was with much regret that the Board approved the sale of those properties."***

By October 1986, all departments of Family First were computerised. Rent accounting went 'live' on August 13th that year.

New-build neighbourhood sites

. . . in Sherwood

A new-build scheme of two two-bedroom houses and four one-bedroom flats was agreed in 1987. This housing was earmarked for people who lived in the Carrington, Sherwood Rise, New Basford, Forest Fields, Mapperley Park or Sherwood areas. The first tenants moved in 1991.

. . . in St Ann's

In 1987/88, Family First received the go-ahead to build homes on two sites in St Ann's intended for people of the St Ann's or nearby Thorneywood districts. These sites were available after the City Council invested Estate Action money in existing Council properties and made parking spaces within gardens. This released infill sites, on land originally earmarked as garage courts, for seven new-build family houses and two bungalows for elderly people. The bungalows released family homes in the area.

Funding was delayed due to Housing Corporation indecision. The properties were completed in 1996.

The changing nature of tenancies and the meaning of 'temporary'

Whilst permanent tenancies were available in Family First's neighbourhood schemes, for some 25 years many of its other properties were available for revolving use by families in urgent need. These homes were called 'temporary' accommodation. They were modernised self-contained flats or houses in a 'normal' housing setting within mixed neighbourhoods (i.e. neither run down nor 'posh'!) with access to amenities. Tenants lived in them, whilst sorting out their – often serious – problems, until they were ready to move into a permanent home, usually a Local Authority home or one belonging to a large housing association. The City Council Housing Department, as mentioned earlier, regarded this process as ideal because, by the time a family was housed by the Local Authority, its problems had usually been satisfactorily resolved. Former Family First tenants tended to become active citizens in their new neighbourhoods, and they retained contact with Family First if they wished to. Many did. Here are a few examples which demonstrate the value of Family First's form of 'temporary' accommodation:-

* A battered wife (1975) was referred to Family First by Social Services. With her two children, she moved into a modern flat in a large converted house with four flats, one of which housed a resident family. The key person in this resident family offered support, links to other services needed and made certain the house was secured at night. The tenant used the day nursery at The Croft for her pre-school age child and spent time with staff when she needed to. She gained confidence and, with Family First's help, secured permanent housing in a district outside Nottingham where she had roots. She never looked back.

* Occasionally, a tenant spends a second spell with Family First. For example, in 1973, Elizabeth Garrod had a three-year-old child and nowhere to live. Nottingham City Council referred her to Family First. She became a tenant until housed permanently. With three children, in 1990 she had to leave a violent relationship. She told the *Nottingham Evening Post* (August 22nd 1996): ***"Family First got me back on my feet as they did almost 20 years earlier. I had grandchildren by then but my life needed sorting out. Like the first time, the same principles applied. No matter what the outside world thought of us, Family First made us feel good about ourselves. It helped stabilise us and helped us all to grow up."***

* The following was one response to a request from the ***Nottingham Evening Post*** for people to write in about their most memorable phone call. Mrs D Askew wrote (1999): ***"The most memorable phone call was the one I made 20 years ago from a phone box to the Family First Trust in Nottingham. The conversation changed my life and the lives of my two small children forever. We were found temporary accommodation and support to rebuild our lives from a volatile and abusive marriage. The scars from that part of our lives have healed over. My children are now grown up and I have grandchildren and a husband who loves me. All thanks to that phone call 20 years ago."***

For many years, the City Housing Department agreed not to exercise its potential right to nominate 50% of tenants to Family First properties because it regarded Family First's innovative and proven work with families as a long-term benefit to its own work.

Family First's concept of 'temporary' housing was, therefore, **very** different from the bed and breakfast 'temporary' accommodation that often was the only available resource for desperate families. Family First's proven successful model of 'temporary' accommodation was not understood by the Housing Corporation. Family First's Housing Manager Brian Kingdom, tried to communicate the facts to the Corporation (1988) when the assured tenancy model was looming in legislation.

Family First had contractual safeguards for tenants in its 'temporary' accommodation which met their actual situation and he added: ***"The success of***

Nottingham's Family First 1965-2005 ISBN 09550948 01

our housing work does depend on a through-put which we achieve with co-operation and active support of Nottingham City Council and other Housing Associations. It is clear that our specialised housing service does not easily fit the current guidelines of Model Agreement for Assured Tenancies in a number of crucial areas." These were then explained in detail but to no avail.

In 1987, Family First had 65 tenancies in 'permanent' accommodation, including 12 families, 34 single people, 15 elders and one couple. It had 109 houses/flats for 'temporary' accommodation. Tenants of these included 78 one-parent families, one elder, 11 single people and four single people with access to children.

'Temporary' accommodation accepted by a one-parent family because they were at a time of crisis was conditional on the parent not taking in a cohabitee. As with the supported tenancies at Mayholme/The Croft, this was not a moralistic condition but a practical one. There was no point in a lone parent wanting accommodation in order to sort life out if, in fact, it was a short cut to another adult taking advantage of a housing opportunity. Very often this condition for 'temporary'accommodation significantly protected a parent from a harassing spouse/partner whilst future decisions were worked out.

The assured tenancy regulations ended Family First's 'temporary' accommodation and thus one of the most effective methods Family First devised for helping families who needed not only housing but support whilst their usually serious difficulties were resolved. This support was offered for as long as necessary within a normal community environment, was tailor-made to suit particular situations, and enabled families eventually to move on confidently, with friendship and informal support networks intact.

The City Council has recently introduced tenancy support for some social housing tenants with problems and uses Family First as one agency to do some of this work. Its tenancy support workers are aware that a big problem faced by many of the families they see is loneliness and isolation. It is ironical that Family First's model of 'temporary' accommodation was introduced as an effective practical way of preventing this problem from ever becoming entrenched.

Most new Family First tenancies since 1989 are full assured tenancies. The exceptions are (a) families or individuals in the rump of 'supported housing' (e.g. Mayholme /The Croft); (b) tenants who have held Family First tenancies since before 1989 and are entitled to a secure tenancy, similar to a full assured one but slightly more beneficial; (c) assured shorthold tenancies used for a small number of market rent housing units (for which different allocation rules apply), and (d) properties leased by Family First with less than 10-year leases remaining.

In 2005, Family First was aiming to make 50% of its vacancies available for nomination by local authorities, including Newark and Sherwood District Council, Mansfield District Council, Nottingham City Council, Gedling Borough Council and Rushcliffe Borough Council.

Family First also sought to commit 24% of vacancies in its bed-sits or one-bedroom flats to young people moving on from hostel projects via Local Authority nominations; its internal waiting list; referrals, or transfers. In this way, Family First continues its special interest in young people.

Housing without strategic long-term thinking?

After Family First's Director Angus Walker left in 1988, growing differences of attitude to the pressures of Housing Corporation policy and practice showed up quite sharply in the Management Committee. From the early 1990s, there was a conflict of view. On the one hand, some members said: ***"Private funding is the order of the day and we must look to whom we house in the context to changing funding"*** or ***"Family First should not be a junior partner in any consortium."*** Others strongly voiced views that there was no benefit in losing a clear sense of direction. In Appendix II, we see the Housing Manager, Brian Kingdom, urging management not to go for growth that did not fit Family First's work. But in its 1995/96 Annual Report Family First stated that its housing development programme: ***"is the third largest amongst Nottingham Housing Associations, made possible by an allocation from the Housing Corporation and reflects the competitive approach of the Association to obtaining funding".***

Pepper-potting

In the 1990s, Family First began to use funding allocations from the Housing Corporation for its imposed purpose of purchasing 'existing satisfactory' properties. It was a difficult housing market. Purchasing single pepper-potted properties (i.e. single properties in a wide variety of locations) within no clearly thought-through long-term strategy created problems for the future. Being satisfactory upon purchase meant immediate use without rehabilitation costs. However, this meant near-future upgrading requirements that could not be budgeted into initial costs. Of course, pepper-pot houses have created homes. Tenants like these houses in some locations, but loathe them in others. Once more, neighbourhood is a key determinant. With hindsight, many of these properties could be described as an expensive distraction to assist short-term Government housing statistics.

Examples of pepper-potted properties considered for purchase at one time in 1994 were (a) a mid-terrace at Snapewood, Bulwell; (b) a City Council-owned terrace house at Crabtree Farm, Bulwell; (c) an ex-Council terrace house in St Ann's, and (d) a house at Bulwell Hall. The last two were brought to Family First's attention by estate agents, anxious to get them off their books. Family First's 1995 Annual Report refers to 20 'existing satisfactories' being included in its development programme funded by the Housing Corporation. The 'existing satisfactory' policy lasted only a few years.

In 1990, Family First was one of four Nottingham housing associations working in an informal consortium with Nottingham Health Authority to provide supported accommodation for people with a history of mental illness. Family First had a shared house for three people, three one-bedroom flats and two two-bedroom ones, and was planning several more. This was an initiative designed to assist the national Care in the Community policy running up to the closure of Mapperley [Psychiatric] Hospital in 1994. The scheme was short-lived. The archives about this are sparse. I cannot prove this, but my belief is that the reason was complicated funding arrangements.

Short-term properties

Family First undertook a short-life housing project at The Old Tracks, 54-58, London Road, formerly The General Gordon pub. It was used for different purposes before (and since). Family First opened it in 1995 on a three-year lease plus a short extension with Nottingham City Council. A £25,000 Housing Corporation short-life grant enabled improvement work done by supervised trainees.

The project was opened by Alan Simpson MP. Six bed-sits and four flats on the floors above the former pub were provided for single people aged over 18 and families. The bars were stripped and the space used for storing furniture for Family First's Furniture Service. Motorists driving along London Road will remember this site because of the colourful murals that Family First painted on boards on the front of the building.

The building was due for demolition in 2005 but it was still there at the year end.

Short-lease properties

Short-lease properties are different from short-life because they will still be housing units when the leases expire. Purchase of a programme of 17 short-lease properties continued into the latter 1990s. Housing Corporation finance was available for part of the cost of rehabilitation of these mostly Local Authority 'difficult' properties. These properties (creating 33 homes) included conversion of shops into flats on the Clifton Estate; on Commercial Road, Bulwell, and in St Ann's.

The ground rent payable (2005) to the City Council on some of the short-lease properties is high: some £800 - £1,000+ p.a.

per housing unit, excluding any service charges.

Since the late 1990s the Family First Board and Executive has tried to address the management and cost problems inherent in some of Family First's housing stock purchased in the early and mid-1990s. Remedy is not possible because of Housing Corporation rules (ever changing) and Local Authority leasehold agreements. Ann Cartwright, Chief Executive, said (2005): ***"The thinking at the time [1990s] seems to have been 'If we don't do what the Local Authority wants, they will not co-operate with us'. When I joined Family First, the Local Authority expected Family First to take on projects like Sneinton Hermitage or converting very unsuitable properties into flats to relieve the Local Authority of problems. That is not what Family First is for."***

West Bridgford Old People's Housing Association

The West Bridgford Old People's Housing Association transferred its assets to Family First in June 1996 after lengthy negotiation. The unregistered association was a charity started by the West Bridgford Round Table some 60 years earlier. Unable to raise funds to refurbish its two substantial houses valued at £250,000 in West Bridgford (a suburb of Nottingham), it transferred them to Family First.

One property was 77, Musters Road with three of its nine flats occupied when a pre-transfer survey was undertaken early in 1996. The other, 55, Melton Road, was a three-storey house with five individual units, but not self-contained. Family First held discussions with Rushcliffe Borough Council about possibilities for the properties.

Existing elderly tenants and the elderly caretaker couple were satisfactorily rehoused. Family First's Furniture Service removed their possessions free of charge, and offered to return and move any furniture in their new homes. A note on file from Age Concern states that Miss M: ***"Had help from two very helpful Family First young men to move her from 77, Musters Road."***

Initially, the property at 77, Musters Road was used temporarily to house tenants from Family First's hostel at 30-32, Waterloo Road, Nottingham, whilst a major refurbishment scheme was carried out. By August 1997, it was decided to refurbish 77, Musters Road as a supported housing project for single homeless people aged over 25 with low support needs. The accommodation then consisted of nine one-bedroom flats (shared bathrooms and toilets) and one self-contained flat. Tenants received practical help, assistance and meals from the Friary Drop-in Centre on Musters Road.

In April 1998, the Mayor of the Borough of Rushcliffe, Geoffrey Kelk, officially opened and named 77, Musters Road 'Swanwick Court' after Councillor Jim Swanwick who founded and chaired the Old People's Housing Association for over 30 years from the mid-1960s.

This project did not last due to funding problems. Rushcliffe Borough Council was unwilling to provide any housing benefit for the support element of the work or to assist under the more recent Supporting People programme. The cost of building improvements to meet the new standards was high. The Board of Family First decided (2001) to sell the property, which closed soon after.

No.55, Melton Road, known as Round Table House, was refurbished in 1999 to provide three one-bedroom and three two-bedroom flats, initially used for move-on independent accommodation for tenants from Swanwick Court. Family First provided tenants with their furniture requirements free of charge from its Furniture Service.

Althea Court, Poyser Close, Basford

This housing complex was built on the site of the demolished Church of St Augustine of Canterbury. Family First initially expressed an interest in 1990. Ann Mitchell, Housing Development Officer, wrote to a Design and Build construction firm: ***"Family First is very interested in the above site for a housing development, with the inclusion of a multi-purpose community room as part of the development: the need for the community facility having been identified by representatives of the local church community.***

"Family First would like to see a two or three-storey development with a mix of two-bedroom houses and one-bedroom flats, preferably slightly more houses than flats. We would ask that two flats and two houses be designed to accommodate people with wheelchairs and that the whole development incorporates features to allow wheelchair access.

"We envisage that the community room would be incorporated structurally into the development, possibly with dwellings above. Ideally, it should be able to hold 75-100 people seated, for worship purposes, and should have a kitchen and toilet facilities with wheelchair access."

For complex and not totally clear reasons, a community room did not happen. It would undoubtedly have been useful in this neighbourhood.

This was the first project for which Family First received loan funding from both the Housing Corporation and from private finance, the Bradford and Bingley Building Society. A bequest from Althea Poyser[3] assisted the release of finance to help this scheme.

Twenty-three homes were built by 1993, consisting of six two-bedroom houses, 13 one-bedroom flats, one two-bedroom flat, and two fully adapted flats for wheelchair users. The majority of tenants came from Nottingham City Council's waiting list.

Family First in Southwell and District

Family First became involved in the Southwell area early in 1974. A Southwell resident, Janet Kirk, requested Family First's help in this minster town some sixteen miles from Nottingham because of decreasing numbers of rented homes and the growing problem of homelessness. She passed a large property to Family First at a generous not-for-profit price due to a legacy she had received. Family First raised a top-up mortgage from the District Council and converted the property into two flats on condition that a local group manage the house. By May 1975, tenants were moving in.

[3] See Bequests

Janet Kirk galvanised voluntary supporters, including Carol Dawson, Judith Milnes, Jeremy and Jennifer Craddock, Daphne Hughes (matron of the local children's home), Susan Santos (who, like Judith Milnes, later joined Family First's Management Committee for some years) and Glenda Brown. The Southwell project was called First Hand, which then registered as the independent Southwell and District Housing Association which raised funds for other local housing projects in the area.

Judith Milnes, a solicitor, said (2004): ***"I was secretary of the Southwell and District Housing Association for some years. Later, I also became a member of the Management Committee of Family First. Those were happy years when it was a small association. It was a pity when Angus Walker left [1988] . . ."*** Judith Milnes became Chairperson of Family First in 1994, following Moira Coles who had served for nine years.

Property prices escalated in the early days of the Southwell and District Housing Association. Its first purchase was a sound ex-Council house that was converted into two flats. The association was savvy and purchased a number of ex-Coal Board houses in the Rainworth and Blidworth areas. Advice was always available from Family First. In 1990, Judith Milnes wrote to Family First requesting ownership transfer of its original Southwell house (which had remained with Family First). The request was refused because the number of properties in ownership of any association was deemed of paramount importance to the Housing Corporation. At that time Judith Milnes said: ***"As is the case with most small and medium-sized housing associations the new grant regime coupled with the Housing Corporation cash crisis has effectively crippled our [Southwell and District Housing Association] development progress."***

In 2004, Judith Milnes told me: ***"In Southwell and District Housing Association, we all worked very hard as volunteers until we employed a part-time administrator. Then the Housing Corporation decided small was not beautiful and wanted us to talk about development only through a larger association."***

1967. One of the then modern bed-sits at The Croft, Alexandra Park, Nottingham: a housing scheme with long-lasting positive outcomes for unsupported young lone mothers (1967 -). See Housing chapter

30-32, Waterloo Road, a pioneer hostel for young people (1981-2005) including those leaving 'care'. The properties were part of Family First's neighbourhood rehabilitation scheme in Waterloo Road and Waterloo Crescent. See Housing chapter

In 1993, the Southwell and District Housing Association (SDHA), which was well run with a part-time administrator and volunteers, transferred its portfolio (including this housing complex in Rainworth) to Family First. The SDHA could no longer remain a small independent housing association because of the Housing Corporation's growing dislike of 'small is beautiful'

Family First building eight flats for elderly people in Mapperley after demolishing a worn-out house in 1974

Houses completed in 1990 by Family First in St Ann's, Nottingham

A housing complex completed by Family First in Basford, Nottingham, in 1993. See Housing chapter which also describes many 'pepper-potted' older properties being purchased at this time

Millennium Court, Basford, built by Family First

The association then undertook a housing scheme through the East Midlands Housing Association before deciding that it would be better to be 'taken over'. The Southwell and District Housing Association approached three housing associations and decided to merge (1993) with Family First with which it ***"had a close relationship for many years".***

The Southwell and District Housing Association brought into Family First's housing portfolio 29 mixed-size refurbished, converted or new build homes, including six two-bedroom flats at Rainworth.

Mobile Holiday Home

In 1995, the Allied Dunbar Foundation purchased a 2/3 bedroom mobile home on the East Coast for Family First to use as a holiday home for members [the title for regulars] using the Crescent Community Centre on Waterloo Road. After the closure of the Community Centre in 1998, the mobile home became used for Family First tenants and was very quickly fully booked. Later the site owners decided they no longer wished to have caravans belonging to charities on site and the caravan was sold for funds.

Millennium Court, Gabriella Close, Basford

The site for this project was a problematic brownfield one assembled following negotiations with three different owners. The resulting (2000) three-storey development created 18 flats, four of which have two bedrooms and are fully adapted for use by tenants with physical disabilities. There are a further two two-bedroom flats and 12 one-bedroom ones.

The local Oakleigh Tenants and Residents' Association was consulted and worked with Family First in the design stage and when the contractors were on site. There was a wish for a well-lit public footpath link between Oakleigh Street and Highbury Road and a public play area for small children. These were achieved and the play area was handed over to Nottingham City Council.

The project was achieved in partnership with the Dudley Building Society, Nottingham City Council and the Housing Corporation.

Some problems have occurred around Millennium Court due to a few people responsible for neighbourhood anti-social behaviour which has involved police co-operation. Considerable effort has been made in creating more tenant involvement in local management of the block, with positive results.

A time to consolidate

Family First has not been purchasing property in the past few years whilst consolidating housing management and finances. As outlined in Appendix II, not all of the £380,000 Housing Corporation allocation for 2002 was taken up because repayments required were not conducive to long-term financial stability.

The Family First Board in 1998 noted that the auditors raised only minor points. However, it was acknowledged that repairs and maintenance were a problem for all housing associations and Family First would take steps to resolve that. Since then, progress has been made to modernise older properties, including, for example, new double-glazed windows, and kitchens. A thorough stock condition survey was carried out in 2004. Between 2005 and 2010, around £1m will be spent on improving Family First's existing homes to meet the required Decent Homes Standards introduced by the Housing Corporation.

As well as selling 30-32, Waterloo Road and 91-93, Waterloo Crescent in 2005, Family First sold several other houses for reasons of inappropriate location or unsuitability for upgrading.

In 2003, the Board decided to convert the former Crescent Community Centre at 34, Waterloo Road into flats. They will be occupied in 2006: one is a social housing flat on the second floor and five are 'for market rent' and occupy the rest of this elegant building.

There is the 40th Anniversary Appeal for £400,000+ for Mayholme/ The Croft (as mentioned earlier in the chapter).

In 2005, the Housing Corporation decided Family First was not a preferred partner as part of its long-term plan to reduce the number of housing associations.

More about tenants

*Family First does not have a tenants' right-to-buy policy. It has always offered advice for tenants wishing to transfer either within or outside Family First's operating area, providing there are no rent arrears. A minority of Family First tenants have been able to purchase a home, especially in the early years when small houses were sometimes affordable for those in work and improvement grants were available to owners. As house prices rose, purchase became more difficult, and schemes have arisen to help. For example, a few Family First tenants benefited from the tenants' incentive scheme, a short-lived Housing Corporation initiative to enable lower-income families to purchase their own homes. Five Family First tenants were in line for this scheme in 1994, having spotted a house they wished to purchase. Family First forwarded their 'case' to the Corporation.

*Tenants with secure or assured tenancies are able to have a lodger or to sub-let a room with permission unless they are in supported housing. Each new tenant receives a clearly written tenant's handbook.

*In 2003/04, 86% of Family First tenants expressed satisfaction with Family First as landlord (7% higher than the national average for registered social landlords). Tenants from ethnic minority communities represented 38.2% of new lettings (national average 14%).

"Family First have treated me as good as they did from the first day I applied for a house. If you have a problem with the home, it is dealt with quickly and efficiently." Tenant (2004).

*Family First reverted in 2002 to streamlining maintenance work by employing an in-house team, including a technical services manager, technical services officer and a cleaning team of two, as well as a direct labour operative with 40 years' experience in the building trade to respond to tenants' needs for routine repairs.

"The Family First staff who have visited my house have been open and friendly and have tried to do the best job they could." Tenant (2005).

*For over 20 of its 40 years, there have been tenant representatives on the Management Committee/Board of Family First. Tenants, in earlier decades, were more often informally linked with members of the Management Committee. For example, they met when community rooms existed at The Croft Family Centre and the Crescent Community Centre. Participation on Management Committees/Boards is not something many tenants choose to do at their current stage in life: informal participation is preferred. Tenants and service users have to be listened to and their ideas taken seriously. With this interpretation of participation, there is much involvement between staff, tenants and service users. But it is not the type of involvement that usually has tick-boxes on official forms!

"I think Mayholme is a good place for people who have problems with being a parent. The staff are easy to approach and very friendly, and they give good advice and support. I find the support sessions useful because I can talk to the staff about any problems I have. I also find that I can have a laugh with the staff. There aren't many places where the staff are so friendly." Norma (2003).

*In September 2003, the ALLPAY system for paying rent by cash/direct debit cards was introduced. Family First's housing office in Clarendon Street, Nottingham, became cash free. This was a security and administration benefit. However, it reduces an occasion for face-to-face meetings. To address this need and the need of tenants to be involved, one action was the appointment (2004) of Tenancy Involvement Worker Andrea Barker. The number of tenants satisfied with opportunities for participating (2005) was 76%.

BEQUESTS

Here are a few examples of individual generosity to Family First through bequests.

Evelyn Hill was prepared to stand firm and speak truth to power when necessary. In the early years of Family First, when there was much public prejudice heaped upon one-parent families, Mrs Evelyn Hill, who lived in Newcastle Drive, The Park, Nottingham, spoke up for the aims, objectives and practice of Family First. She was much respected in the city and beyond. After she died, I wrote a letter to the *Nottingham Evening Post,* May 23rd, 1990 stating: ***"From the very start [of Family First] Evelyn Hill gave of her time, love and support and did a great deal to change attitudes in the city. Sometimes, when my colleagues and I were despairing, she would offer that shoulder to cry on which is so healing and which gives the energy to continue . . .***

"Prejudices have changed a little, but the need for a home not at all. . . . Evelyn Hill in her request 'No flowers, money to Family First' recognised that the problem has not gone away. Her witness, especially for homeless mothers, was long, loving and practical."

Yvonne Lucy Howett left a legacy of £20,000* to Family First in 2004/05. Family First was the main beneficiary from Mrs Howett's will and there were no stipulations as to how the money should be used.

Gertrude May Zita Lewis of 22, Bedale Road, Sherwood, died on November 8th, 1992. Her executor, Harrison, Golds & Rushworth, solicitors, said she bequeathed all her personal chattels to two friends who, after selecting a few items of sentimental interest but 'no particular value', asked that the rest should be sold and the proceeds given to Family First. The two friends were Mrs J Brown of Gotham, Nottinghamshire, and Mr J Allred of Boston Spa, West Yorkshire. The net proceeds were £189.94.

Althea Mary Poyser of Attenborough died on September 18th, 1989. She bequeathed one-fifth of her residual estate to Family First. This amounted to £49,596.47. This finance enabled release of private funds from the Bradford and Bingley Building Society (plus Housing Corporation loan) to build 23 houses and flats on the site of the demolished St Augustine of Canterbury Church, Basford, Nottingham. Her sister Marjorie Poyser agreed that the housing complex could be named after her late sister, providing her Christian name Althea was used ***"in order to avoid confusion with any other Poyser family in Nottingham".***

Marjorie Poyser initiated the project by 'digging' the first soil in 1992. Afterwards, she wrote: ***"The hospitality at The Fox was very welcome on such a cold day."*** Family First presented her with a ***"handsome spade and a beautiful basket of flowers."*** She added: ***"I am sure the work you are all doing would be very pleasing to my sister Althea."*** Althea's executors were her sister and two well-known Nottingham people, David Corder and Sidney Basil Treece. **Marjorie Poyser** left a legacy of £75,000* to Family First in 2004.

Lorna Mary Wilkinson in the early 1970s was seeking a suitable voluntary housing organisation to offer a life-time gift of £54,000: a very substantial sum then. She lived in Berkshire and wished to remain anonymous in her lifetime. I was interviewed by her solicitor before she made the gift to Family First. The donor paid several private visits to The Croft to watch 14 flats on adjoining land being built: a project her money made possible. She told me she had been very fortunate in life and wished the £54,000 to provide homes for people who had none. She specifically said she did not mind if the future tenants had experienced major life problems of their own making (e.g. going to prison) providing having a home and support enabled them to ***'come through'***. The flats were called Lorna Court and Mary Court after her given names.

Lorna Mary Wilkinson died in 1993. In deciding how to allocate further money she wished to leave Family First in her will, her son asked Family First Director Graham Wright for a 'wish list' of what was needed. He concluded his reply with: ***"Housing and homelessness for young people are a major problem and there are not too many people around prepared to give in the way your mother did."***

* These legacies have been placed in the 40th Anniversary Appeal fund to assist the rehabilitation of Mayholme/The Croft or its replacement in a new venue. This project for young lone mothers was Family First's first owned housing project.

Prince Charles visited the Action Resource Centre in Nottingham on February 18th, 1988. Its local Director, John Pike, insisted that the Prince's itinerary include the Family First training workshops because of the "excellence of the work being carried out". A letter of thanks from the Palace said how much the Prince enjoyed his visit and how refreshing it was to meet "real people". Photo courtesy of the Nottingham Evening Post. See Training and Trainees chapter

 Nottingham's Family First 1965-2005 ISBN 09550948 01

FAMILY FIRST ASSISTED

Parents Anonymous

Maria Dabrowska, community worker at Family First, and a small team of volunteers including Dr Sandra Buck, a volunteer neighbour of Family First's Croft Family Centre, started Parents Anonymous in the Nottingham area on November 1st, 1976. It was a parents' self-help idea from America but new in the UK. The Nottingham adaptation was for parents to be able to contact a telephone line in confidence if experiencing problems with their children (including abuse).

Maria Dabrowska told me (2005): ***The project seemed an incredibly courageous thing to do. We were on the crest of a wave of people understanding that technology was available for these things . . . the Family First environment was so supportive. We had to make up our own training and preparation programme. We went to Telephone Samaritans for help, to Social Services and to health visitors. They didn't have all the answers because it hadn't been done before . . . It started with a group of seven volunteers who were totally committed."*** It was possible to place a British Telecom central phone at Family First and then each night of the week, from 6 p.m. to midnight, the phone was switched to a trained volunteer's home.

"We were involved with a third party who was the child," said Maria. ***"So the danger was that if abuse was happening and we didn't do the right thing, it might end with the death of a child. Everything we did and our preparation programme was to know how to pick up on the danger signals and know what to do***." Many agencies, including the NSPCC, were available to help. There was no big publicity to begin with so the number of calls started very slowly and the team developed its skills. Eventually, a group of parents who had phoned in met each other. ***"It was very hard work because self-help is hard work. The parents worked on their relationships with their children, and some of those parents became volunteers,"*** said Maria.

Later the BBC made a programme about Parents Anonymous. Many people were becoming more socially aware. Parents Anonymous became Parent Line and set up a national co-ordinating group for the growing number of local groups of ordinary concerned parents. They were years of much hard work.

Eventually, Esther Rantzen set up Child Line with huge national publicity and the focus of interest changed to child centred help.

Maria Dabrowska still believes that in order to help children their parents need help. She says: ***"While there are a few parents who are psychopaths who actually enjoy torturing their children, the vast majority are just stuck and in trouble. I still don't think that their everyday needs are being met in terms of community support. Most parents want to have a good relationship with their children."***

Home-Start Nottingham

Home-Start came to Nottingham in 1979. Family First actively encouraged it. Until it was viable, it used office space in the Director, Angus Walker's office at The Croft, Alexandra Park. Angus told me (2004) that both Home-Start and Parents Anonymous were projects with the same basic principles as Family First. These included an absolute belief that all people are equal, the value of self-help and volunteers, and having an unpatronising approach to life.

Nottingham Home-Start was set up to help and support families with pre-school children where the family unit was experiencing problems. It spread to other areas of Nottinghamshire. It is very active today. For more information see www.home-startnottingham.org.uk.

The Croft Family Centre, including a day nursery, opened in 1975 and extended Family First's community based work at The Croft. Here, a 'family group' in the day nursery is having a meal in one of four rooms with flexible partitions leading to a large hall. Through the window is one outside play area and Lorna Court and Mary Court (opened 1974 and 1975) for mixed housing, including for single-parent families

A group of some of the children and staff at The Croft Family Centre day nursery taking part in their annual group photo (1988)

NEIGHBOURHOOD CENTRES

From the time in 1965/66 when Family First owned the adjoining properties Mayholme/The Croft in Alexandra Park, Nottingham, the ground floor was used both as a neighbourhood centre and as the base for Family First's city-wide work. The description 'neighbourhood centre' was not used then, but the concept of creating projects within a neighbourhood context, and not in isolation, was never negotiable.

Below, I outline the role and achievements of Family First's neighbourhood centres. Their story also demonstrates the increasingly difficult 'official' climate that confronts inclusive community self-help which is independently minded.

Community space at Mayholme/The Croft 1965-1975

Even before young lone pregnant or new mothers moved into the upstairs modern flatlets in The Croft, the ground floor was put to use. With a large Community Room, a general purpose room, office and kitchen, Family First had a base to which families and individuals came to seek help. Many people, including neighbours, volunteers, students, trainees and Family First tenants already housed in the city, used The Croft as a meeting point and for events.

I recall preparing large quantities of food for celebrations in the Community Room, including tenant get-togethers over the Christmas period. Funds were tight. The food was often 'bangers and mash' served in a festively decorated room until Peter Elderfield from Coalville called before Christmas each year with a huge turkey he reared. He founded the East Midlands Housing Association.

I will not dwell too much on the richness of experience in, and stemming from, The Croft over the early years[1]. It influenced much that has happened in Family First, and what people have taken from it into their future work and life in many places.

One mother, who in the late 1960s had three young children and a husband with a severe disability, wrote (2005): ***"We were often quite desperate financially, Christmas especially. It was an early encounter with Family First when 'Father Christmas' quietly arrived with a sack full of toys. I will never forget that. There were other surprises in the next few years. My rotting draining board was replaced and a bed came for a child, and a number of willing workers appeared to do urgent jobs. There were social events we all went to with singing and dancing [at The Croft].***

"I went on to help Family First in various ways, for example by giving talks. There was never a feeling that one was 'being done good to': volunteers and beneficiaries met in friendship and sharing, as well as what I'd call 'celebration' for the atmosphere was like that. To me, Family First was a wonderful beacon of hope." RJ, who became a home teacher.

The Croft Family Centre 1975-2005

Extracts from a 1972 paper on the proposed use of The Croft Family Centre (opened 1975) is in Appendix I. It outlines aims of the Family Centre and how it would enhance then current work at The Croft.

The Family Centre was built adjoining Mayholme/The Croft. The name 'family centre' is now commonly used but was then new. Family First's Family Centre included a 30-place day nursery. A new large kitchen enabled meals to be prepared not only for the nursery children, but also – as a community café – for anyone involved with Family First including neighbours. The laundry room in the day nursery had coin-operated machines. In the evenings and at

[1] This has been written about in *Life Goes On*. See footnote on page 3

weekends, it became a neighbourhood launderette, just as the pay phone in The Croft had long served the local community (no mobile phones then). The day nursery had outside play space back and front. Out of hours, the front area was used by under-fives living in the 14 new flats on the site. Some years later, all the nursery play area was moved to the back.

The day nursery had a large hall with four 'family' rooms leading off, each with a folding door to draw across for rest and mealtimes and in the evenings to safeguard children's work and toys when the hall was used by a youth club. There was a baby room, indoor water and sand play area, cloakroom, office and welcoming parent space.

The Croft Family Centre was running for some weeks before it was officially opened on September 13th, 1975 by Margaret Bramall, Director of the Council for One Parent Families. She said the Family Centre would be inspirational far and wide: it showed what was possible. The Croft Family Centre was funded by a Government urban aid capital grant and a five-year revenue grant. The costs of running a day nursery are high because of the ratio of trained staff needed. Good child care for pre-school children, universally available to parents in some western countries, has always been a vexed issue in the UK: it still is.

The first Family Centre Manager was Ann Stephenson, already a community worker with Family First. Hers was a unique post nationally at the time. Tenant, neighbour and volunteer participation expanded quickly. Five regular part-time volunteers were soon responsible to Ann Stephenson as well as occasional helpers. The team of qualified nursery nurses added a lot of energy to the Family Centre. Ann Stephenson was eventually replaced by Joy McLaughlin. Next came Gill Howell-Jones (formerly Keyse). The current post-holder, Carmen Barnes (nee McPherson), worked as Child Care Supervisor with Gill Howell-Jones.

When the Family Centre opened, among the 26 Family First tenants on the site were a nursery nurse (in The Croft); the Family Centre Manager and her son (in Mary Court); the site Caretaker and his son (in Lorna Court), and myself and three children. From the early 1970s I was paid as Director of Family First but remained voluntary resident family at The Croft. Only the caretaker was paid for residential responsibilities. Mine were considerable; the other two resident staff assisted on occasions, and helped to provide a sense of continuity and security. We all paid rent. There was a real sense of community, including occasional crises, such as sudden illness of a child and the attempted suicide of a newly arrived expectant mother whose elder child had recently been murdered.

The small purpose-built office block at the entrance of The Croft housed the reception office; housing manager; accounts office and personal services manager. My office was in the 'old' Croft building. Work was a blend of serious planning and business, practical daily issues and the unexpected. Sometimes they all blended.

Everyone felt involved

When a battered wife arrived in the Community Room in distress, a pregnant 16-year-old sat her down in a chat-corner, made her a cup of tea and talked with her until she calmed, then made sure she was seen by a relevant member of staff. This was no isolated instance. Everyone felt involved. That ethos does not happen by chance. The Family Centre included all ages, including pensioners who had a Luncheon Club.

A diverse mix of children at the day nursery included some whose families were experiencing complex and serious problems. The day nursery held events for families; courses on parenting; open days for everyone; outings for the children, and lots more. For security, anyone entering the day nursery went through nursery reception. There were many occasions when people involved in the nursery took part in the wider life of the Family Centre, whether for mother and toddler groups, social events or simply enjoying a meal or a cup of tea and chatting to a friend.

Neighbours added a huge dimension to life at The Croft Family Centre. There was, for example, Louis, a 1956 refugee from Hungary and an engineer. He lived nearby

Nottingham's Family First 1965-2005 ISBN 09550948 01

and ran an allotment from which he supplied neighbours (including Croft tenants) with free fresh vegetables. He invited everyone to a bonfire each November 5th which included ash-roasted jacket potatoes. He mended prams and pushchairs. There were many families, and couples, in the neighbourhood who both helped and enjoyed Family First amenities. Skilled neighbours sometimes befriended a young mother needing confidence to develop personal and parenting skills. Such links were a choice, never mandatory, which is why they usually worked so well. Some friendships thus made still exist.

1980s and 1990s

In the mid-1980s the day nursery was still registered for 30 children attending at any one time, and registered for up to eight children attending the playgroup in another room. By the time the Centre was 15 years old, its staff were continuing to support local community groups and were represented on the Management Committees/Governing Boards of the local primary school, Playworks, the Toy Library Federation and Home-Start.

In 1990, police officers barbecued food for the 200 adults and children who attended the annual Croft Family Centre summer event. Parents' evenings were held regularly throughout the year. Subjects included learning through play, the national curriculum and child development. There were discos and social events. The Croft kitchen continued to provide a focal point and meals and snacks at reasonable cost. Emphasis on healthy eating and multi-cultural foods formed an integral part of the menus and proved popular.

In 1992, 80 families were helped with full or part-time day care, and after-school and holiday care. The kitchen services, toy library and toddler groups supported a considerable number more. Nelsons Solicitors donated £1,600 towards new outdoor play equipment. The users of the Family Centre raised £300.

The next year, nursery officers (who were formerly called nursery nurses and are now called family workers) completed "Myself" books with all the children to celebrate their individual family and lifestyle. The day nursery was then registered for 34 children. It served a mixture of families, including those who needed child care in order to work or train, and those who needed it because of some difficulty. The general purpose room was used for after-school care, toddler groups, book and toy library, and the Family Centre remained a drop-in point for the local community.

The Croft Family Centre evolved positively and steadily, but during the mid-1990s, a decision of then Management Committee and Director (Graham Wright) significantly altered the way in which tenants, neighbours, trainees and volunteers were able informally to meet each other. The wonderful Community Room was divided into offices. On the first floor, tenants were moved across to Mayholme to make way for more offices. This followed changes of housing staff that provoked opposition of other staff and, importantly, of tenants. These actions followed pressure from the Housing Corporation for Family First to develop as a 'general' housing association: pressure, evident in the Housing chapter and Appendix II, which the Management Committee for a short period accepted.

The much smaller general purpose room was re-designated the 'community room'!

When Ann Cartwright became Family First's Chief Executive in 1997, its administration was scaled down. In 2000, its central administration and housing offices moved to the site of Family First's Furniture and Clothing Service in Alfred Street North. This reinstated space for three more tenants upstairs at Mayholme/The Croft. The former large Community Room was not reinstated and might not have worked if it had. It is very easy to destroy community participation. It can grow and evolve only from solid roots and cannot be imposed. The divided-up space, however, was reclaimed for active work with families linked to the Family Centre and day nursery, for mother and toddler groups, parenting groups and more recently a safe contact centre.

The Croft Family Centre staff continued to create ways to do their best for the families using the Family Centre's day nursery and other services. Proof of this came, in 1996, when Family First was the recipient of Nottinghamshire County Council's largest voluntary sector grant. Nottinghamshire County Council recognised the extent of the benefit to the local community of Family First's work. In particular, it recognised The Croft Family Centre as a high quality provider of child care and family support. The County Council was fully aware, due to its own diligence, of problems in the central/housing administration of Family First in the mid-1990s, but this did not affect the County Council's respect for or support of Family First's practical work and, in particular, its day nursery[2].

In 1994, the County Council re-designated all its own Social Services day nurseries as family centres. In the Children's Act 1989, local authorities were given more duties to promote the upbringing of children by their own families through provision of family support. The type of integrated family work that Family First had been practising and developing for several decades therefore became in theory more generally accepted. Family First also had the inherent advantage of having its Family Centre adjacent to some if its supported housing.

The Croft Family Centre registered with OFSTED [Office for Standards in Education] in 1994 and has always received very positive reports. In 2003, for example, when the day nursery was registered for 38 children aged 0 – eight years, there were 35 children on roll. Day care provision was from 8.00 a.m. to 6.00 p.m. Monday to Friday, 50 weeks a year. Seven qualified full-time staff were employed to work with the children plus an officer-in-charge. The inspection report makes it clear that children, including those with special needs, were well cared for in all respects, including the provision of nutritious food that complied with dietary and religious requirements. Parents were obviously made welcome and fully aware of their child's progress.

Sunday breakfasts at The Croft Family Centre happened once a month in the mid-1990s. Around 80 people enjoyed a good inexpensive meal and time to relax and play. For two years, around 25 parents and their children took a joint holiday at Champion House in Edale, Derbyshire, having saved sometimes all year to do so.

In partnership with Walter Halls School, in 1995 Family First worked to obtain City Challenge and Greater Nottingham TEC funding to relocate its after-schools care provision formerly undertaken at The Croft Family Centre. The move would enable 24 children to be cared for at Walter Halls School premises.

All appropriate staff undertook in-house training (1995) to respond positively to the child protection guidelines of the Nottinghamshire Area Child Protection Committee. Priority was placed on strengthening existing links with Nottinghamshire Social Services Department, resulting in the formal provision of 10 child care/family support places at the Family Centre day nursery. The Family Centre had growing demand for family support work from social workers and health visitors making referrals. In addition to individual support and counselling, the Family Centre ran twice weekly family support sessions and parenting skills courses. This family support was acclaimed by other agencies and The Centre decided to focus on developing this work. Also, in view of the Children's Act 1989 it took steps to include more children with special needs through provision of short-term respite care.

In 1996, there was a 'dramatic expansion' of family support services particularly through the provision of parenting skills courses. Here are some participants' comments. (1) ***"I'm really starting to enjoy my kids now."*** (2) ***"Basically I don't shout at them so much. I don't smack them. I discuss things more with them."*** (3) ***"Helped me feel better about myself."*** (4) ***"Meeting other parents and sharing experiences has been great."*** Parent/carer consultation sessions and information evenings became regular features.

[2] I discovered this when I researched records of Nottinghamshire County Council's Voluntary Sector Support Unit prior to Nottingham City Council regaining unitary status in 1998

Nottingham's Family First 1965-2005 ISBN 09550948 01

A sum of £10,000 was received from BBC Children in Need to provide additional play space at The Croft Family Centre in 1996/97. For the first time, the day nursery was open 52 weeks a year (expect for Bank Holidays and three training days) 7.30 a.m. to 6.00 p.m., with nursery places on full, part-time or sessional basis. Fifty-five families used the day nursery.

At this time, the nursery stated it was caring for babies aged six weeks to two years; kindergarten for two-year-olds, and pre-school group for three and four-year-olds. It was a registered nursery education provider. All special needs could be met. The nursery was available for self-supporting lone parent/carers (66%) who were working or training; 'children in need' including children with disabilities (16%); tenancy support places (2%), and private places (16%). A total of 84 children were cared for. The staff/child ratios were in excess of recommendations in the Children's Act 1989. The nursery was registered for a maximum of 34 children per day. It had a manager, deputy manager, child care supervisor, senior family worker, three family workers, and four assistant family workers.

In addition, the developing family support services helped 69 families. Of these, 22% took part in family support sessions; 20% in one-to-one counselling; 32% in the drop-in facilities, and 26% in parenting skills courses.

Councillor Tony Robinson, Sheriff of Nottingham, opened an extension to The Croft Family Centre day nursery which provided an additional baby room (1998) funded by the BBC's Children in Need Appeal donation.

A major review of fees and admission structures was undertaken to ensure that services continued to be provided in the most effective way for those who needed them most, i.e. a moving towards a policy of increasing the number of 'children in need' (1999). OFSTED inspection report 1999 stated: ***"The Croft Family Centre provides a stimulating and friendly environment for children's learning . . . Behaviour is very good and children work well both independently and in groups. Cultural awareness and sensitivity to others are encouraged through a strong programme of celebrations."***

Additionally, the day nursery's Early Years inspection report for 1999 said: ***"The staff were observed to give children lots of appropriate attention through play, verbal communication and affection. Staff encouraged the children to play and sample the range of activities that were on offer, using these opportunities to develop and enhance the children's level of concentration, intellect and social skills . . ."***

From 2000

In 2000, The Croft Family Centre responded to the introduction of the Working Family Tax Credit by undertaking discussions concerning the possible impact on Local Authority funding of subsidised child care. The matter remained unresolved. After considering all options, Patrick Taylor, Family First's Director of Community Resources and Support Services, said (2003) that Gill Howell-Jones, Service Head of the Family Centre, felt there was no possibility of the day nursery breaking even financially because of the new way families were being 'helped' with child care costs (see also next section).

A trained male member of The Croft Family Centre staff developed (1999/2000) an identity course to support young males aged eight to14 years with negative or no adult male role models.

The next year saw a reduction in the number of children in the day nursery. By 2002, it was described as a unique resource in the child care community through its ability to deal with some of the most vulnerable and challenging children. It expanded its community based activities by rejigging some of the space into a cosy community room with a toy library. A sensory and therapeutic room for children with disabilities or special educational needs was installed in the day nursery and paid for by the BBC's Children in Need Appeal fund. And a soft playroom was added.

"David was referred to us by Social Services as a child in need. He needed help in learning to play and with keeping himself clean. Conditions at home were so poor in

terms of hygiene and safety that the family had to be rehoused. David came to the nursery for two days a week so that we could monitor his welfare and so that his mother could have some respite support following the death of her partner. At present David comes to the nursery regularly and his health and general development have improved." Staff member (2003).

The intricate weaving of individual patterns of day care and family support are a huge responsibility for staff. One morning (2004) I was at the Family Centre when a family worker visited a child's home because the child had not arrived at the day nursery and there was no phone contact. The child was found in the sole care of the father who was severely intoxicated.

Family workers' help is almost always appreciated. The majority of referrals come from social workers, with health visitors and Portage workers also making good use of the services. Within all Family First services, there is the opportunity for self-referral.

The day nursery caters for babies to school-age children. Nutritious breakfasts, snacks, lunches and teas are still provided. The nursery has a large outdoor play area and is in a district with clean air. Despite all the family difficulties represented, life at the Family Centre is remarkably relaxed and the everyday simple things are valued, such as the 2005 January Newsletter which explains the topics that the children will be focusing on in the day nursery. There are plenty of ideas for parents and children to work on at home following the topics, e.g. making a weather chart. But – to the casual onlooker – the depth of the work undertaken might be overlooked, because it looks totally normal.

In 2004/05, referrals of the children receiving child care at The Croft Family Centre day nursery, many on a sessional basis, came from Social Services (69); self-referral (12); health visitors (129); via Mayholme/The Croft or tenancy support (65); private (9), and others (3). The longest-serving Family Centre members of staff are Jackie Schofield, Senior Administrative Officer, who joined Family First in 1989 and Doreen Virtue. She started in June 1994 as a family worker and is now a Grade 2 Family Worker with some senior responsibilities. Doreen is also the Special Educational Needs Co-ordinator.

In summer 2005, the annual Fun Day at The Croft Family Centre celebrated Family First's four decades. Ian West (cook at The Croft Family Centre) made a yummy 40th anniversary cake.

Interface with statutory policies

Here I want to record important changes which altered the mix of children using Family Centre resources including the day nursery.

It was in 1986 when The Croft Family Centre Manager, Gill Keyse (later Howell-Jones), reported that the changing nature of referrals to the day nursery meant less preventative work and increasingly helping families at crisis point. Staff experienced the effects of stress caused by this because, for example, it created the need for more part-time attendances at the nursery. The Chairman of Family First's Management Committee's Housing and Community Services Sub-Committee, the Revd Paul Watts, said at the time: ***"The Family First Family Centre is the only voluntary scheme in mainstream funding providing such a service and all agree on the skilful way in which teamwork is being carried out within the nursery."*** The Committee agreed it would ***"support the nursery accepting fewer children in order to maintain the current excellence of service".***

At the beginning of 1987, there was further consideration of the balance of children using the day nursery. June Allen, Senior Professional Adviser for under fives with Nottinghamshire County Council, stressed the need for Family First to continue offering a service to working parents. The Croft Family Centre Support Group considered this to be a vital role and Family First should resist any attempts to change into a crisis-only centre. Nottinghamshire County Council, a key funder, perceived that the day nursery's role should not be limited to families with extreme problems, because it was not in their best interests to be isolated but to be included in a diverse group.

From the inception of The Croft Family Centre, the County Council recognised that the Centre's preventative and positive policy

Nottingham's Family First 1965-2005 ISBN 09550948 01

was valuable. The Council liked not only the nursery's mix of children from diverse ethnic backgrounds but also socio-economic backgrounds (i.e. working and non-working parents). The mix of children also included a wide range of abilities and needs. The County Council understood and valued the fact that the Family Centre's work represented good value for money. But times were changing and, as we saw in the section above, by 1995 Nottinghamshire Social Services Department had specifically reserved ten child care/family support places at the Family Centre. Increasingly, central Government policies and local authorities' ambivalence about their own role were having a local impact of policy uncertainty.

As we have also seen earlier, 1996 was the year when the County Council granted Family First its largest voluntary sector grant. It endorsed Family First's preventative and inclusive community work, including within its day nursery. But this positive vision faded as increasing funding uncertainties stemmed from a coincidence of factors. These included changes to local authority structures resulting in Nottingham City Council regaining unitary status (1997/98). This was also the time when The Croft Family Centre received validation as a nursery education provider which coincided with the introduction of the national Nursery Voucher Scheme. A number of Family First nursery users chose to use their vouchers at the local school which – like many primary schools – geared up to taking children of a younger age. This followed a national trend of more parents believing that 'education' in a school setting would be in the best interests of their pre-school children.

Nottingham City Council undertook consultation with family centres about their services. Family First was involved in the process through Gill Howell-Jones, Service Head of The Croft Family Centre, and Carmen McPherson (later Barnes), its Service Manager. There is no space to detail all the subtle changes that followed. The language of managing services has become, I believe, difficult for the general public to engage with. For example, in one City Council document (2000) outlining the aims of the City's family centres to meet objectives for children's services of the City's Social Services Department and of Government, the 11th objective was: ***"To maximise the benefits of service users from the resources available, and to demonstrate the effectiveness and value for money of the care and support provided and to allow choice and different responses to different needs and circumstances."*** I frequently meet people who, when confronted by similar language, state simply: ***"Yes, but what does that actually MEAN?"***

Changing public funding of child care costs at the turn of the 21st century meant The Croft Family Centre day nursery changed from a nursery for a whole spectrum of children with parents being involved to a Family Centre offering parent support (with the day nursery as 'tool' for helping a group of children who became officially known by statutory authorities as 'children in need').

If low-income working families wished to use the nursery, it became increasingly difficult for them to do so. From October 2004, Croft Family Centre staff were seeking clarification about how a new system for calculating child care costs on Family Credit benefit payments might be worked out. In reply to a letter from Gill Howell-Jones, the Benefits Agency wrote (13.10.94):***"What is quite clear is that: (a) no one will benefit by £40 a week; (b) very few will benefit by the actual maximum of £28 a week, and (c) a lot of people will not benefit at all. What is happening in practice is that Family Credit is offsetting Child Care costs against earnings before calculating entitlement. The 70% taper means, of course, that £3 in every £10 comes off the Family Credit amount, so people will still have to find part of the child care themselves.***

"More importantly those already receiving maximum Family Credit will not gain at all. I realise that this matter is of great concern to you."

The fragmentation of different routes of funding for the provision of pre-school child care adds to family stress and problems. There is no clear message about the advantage of good quality child care (whatever parents' circumstances) and the need to regard it as a national social cost. As an instance of the current confusion, in 2005 the Low Incomes Tax Reform Group spent several weeks dissecting the tax credit system and the voucher scheme to see where they overlapped, and how the trade-offs between the two would operate for families.

The loneliness and needs of many families today can be symptoms of a society in which neighbourhoods and/or extended families often do not have the self-help capabilities that are necessary and desirable. Social policies often exacerbate this lack. In our current culture, as a generalisation, you are officially perceived as EITHER a 'capable' (i.e. self-sufficient) person/ family able to determine and fund a materially secure life OR you are viewed as 'vulnerable' and maybe needing 'special help'. Yet, Family First's experience is that families and individuals defy such generalisations. A family can be both vulnerable and, in some ways, competent at the same time. It can both need help and be able to offer it.

But today's reality is that 'children in need' are separated through imposed social policies, and they and their families cannot be allowed to drop off the edge. Family First's Chief Executive, Ann Cartwright, reminded Nottingham City Council of this when it stated, without prior consultation and in contravention of the contractual notice period, that it would reduce funding for The Croft Family Centre day nursery by over two-thirds in 2005/06.

Ann Cartwright wrote to Social Services (April 2005): ***"This funding crisis within your department has come without any prior warning or consultation and is completely contrary to the principles of the Voluntary and Community Sector Compact and partnership working, as well as the principles of 'Every Child Matters'. These problems were not mentioned at our recent meetings with staff from the Commissioning Team to discuss and agree a new Service Level Agreement for The Croft Family Centre. In fact, at these meetings, rather than looking for cuts in the levels of services being delivered by us, we were asked to rewrite part of the Service Level Agreement to include an increase in the level of service we could provide . . .***

"As far as we are aware, we are the only provider of services to children and families designated as 'Children in Need' within the City. How do Social Services now intend to discharge their statutory duty of care to these children and at what cost? If it is your intention to spot-purchase this specialist provision from other sources outside of the City, how does this demonstrate 'Best Value' or 'Value for Money?' . . . Who pays the redundancy costs for staff we will be forced to make redundant as a result of these cuts?" At the time over 30 children used The Croft Family Centre day nursery each week.

Letters for continuation of the full support of Social Services came from health visitors, Social Services family support workers, and the Team Leader of the City of Nottingham Local Education Authority's Portage and Early Education Team. As had happened before, the Local Authority grass-roots workers greatly valued and needed Family First whilst, as a funding body, the Local Authority could arbitrarily fail even to consult properly.

The Team Leader, Portage and Early Education, wrote (2005): ***"As a home visiting service, we often develop close relationships with families. The children that we work with have Special Educational Needs and often need a high level of supervision and care. At times it can be difficult for families to feel that they are able to cope with the needs of all of their children. Some families experience difficult or traumatic circumstances.***

"I know that families have really appreciated the time and care that your service [Family First Family Centre day nursery] has provided for them . . . I hope that you will be able to support children and their families in future."

In May 2005, Social Services retreated from their former position and decided to finance 'existing arrangements' for 2005/06.

Nottingham's Family First 1965-2005 ISBN 09550948 01

The Croft Family Centre now

It is a huge tribute to The Croft Family Centre staff that they steadfastly take a holistic approach to what is possible for each child and each family. As pots of funding become available, projects are added to what can be offered, such as tenancy support and a safe contact centre (see below). But, in order to provide a holistic range of services, there is constant insecurity about how long funding will last. How may it be possible to create continuity so essential for families in crisis? However, by also having supported housing and other services, Family First has useful flexible tools which creatively assist in some situations, as Maria's story below indicates.

In 2005, the day nursery was used entirely for children referred by Social Services.

Kate Duke, Manager of the Family Centre, told me (2005) that children might attend the nursery for several sessions a week to give respite to parents struggling to cope with their children's behaviour. Examples of problems include routines for sleeping, eating, weaning, toileting, whilst there are family difficulties such as mental health, relationship, budgeting, and housing. So the family workers will support families whilst encouraging a child's development at the nursery.

"The Croft Family Centre is unique," Kate believes because a family can be helped to get on its feet through Family First's 'family' of services. For example, in the Mayholme/The Croft hostel, a mum can be helped with parenting support whilst her child attends the day nursery for several sessions a week. Once the family has gained skills and is ready for its own independent accommodation, Family First can help there. Then there may be a need to support with budgeting plans or help to obtain furniture or children's items (again within Family First through the Furniture Service and Kidstuff).

"You never get one family that's the same as another," said Kate Duke. ***"I've noticed since the closure of some of the Council's family centres in Nottingham that are funded through Social Services that our referrals have changed. We are having more children referred who are on the child protection register."***

Maria's story

I met Maria at one of Family First's 40th anniversary celebrations. She told me her story and hopes it may help someone else. Maria is an intelligent mother who now has a bright future and so do her children. It could well have been otherwise, but for her determination to use the flexible help available through Family First.

Maria started drinking when she was 14 and was alcoholic until she was 21. Her alcohol addiction built up slowly and she said: ***"It's an easy thing to hide for a long time."*** Her two young sons were taken 'into care'. Two years ago when her life was ruined through drinking, she became pregnant by a man who was violent. Her own birth family cut its links with her. The City Council Social Services Department referred her to the Family First Mayholme hostel. There she had a comfortable bed-sit that became her home. ***"I arrived with only the track-suit I was wearing,"*** she said.

She spoke highly of the staff who supported her and she attended a clinic to address her addiction. Her daughter was born healthy and was able to attend the Family First day nursery next door twice a week during the time Maria was turning her life around. She now lives with her daughter in a nearby independent Family First flat. Her daughter has come off the child protection register.

Maria's birth family and Maria are reconciled. Her sons' father has custody of them, but she has earned the right to have regular contact with them both, including their staying overnight. Maria has booked herself into a parenting class.

It is too easy for young people to get addicted to alcohol, says Maria, who now looks with sorrow at underage teenagers who can so easily purchase it with no questions asked.

Tenancy support project

In 2003, tenancy support was added to services offered by The Croft Family Centre. It is an outreach service. A team of six tenancy support workers each support a group of Nottingham city social housing tenants to help them feel confident to cope with problems. These include debt management, housing repairs, benefit payments and family crisis. The service is funded through the Government's Supporting People initiative. Most of the families are referred by health visitors, Social Services, St Ann's Family Centre, from within Family First, and some are self-referrals. One of the key problems within families supported is isolation and loneliness.

Family First is one of several agencies undertaking this work and it tends to support one-parent families (but not exclusively). For example, it has helped parents of six children, two of whom had severe learning difficulties. In 2004/05, 112 people received support. Each visit to a family usually lasts from 50-90 minutes once or twice a week. There are 33 families being supported at any one time. Help is not indefinite: the aim is to assist confident independence. A few comments from those supported:-

(1) ***"I thought it was me against the world until I met . . . Just knowing somebody cares enough to give a little help and support means a lot."*** (2) ***"I have calmed down a lot."*** (3) ***" . . . has been brilliant with us and the kids. She's never looked down her nose at us."***

Supervised safe contact centre

In November 2004, a room was prepared at The Croft Family Centre as a welcoming supervised safe contact centre to enable parents separated from their children, often due to violence, to meet in an informal, safe and supportive environment. At present this is the only such centre in the county. There is much demand for this service and already a waiting list.

Crescent Community Centre

The Crescent Community Centre, at 34, Waterloo Road, was a large detached property in Family First's neighbourhood rehabilitation scheme on Waterloo Road and Waterloo Crescent. Much renovation and conversion work inside the building was done by trainees, with skilled supervision, from Family First's training schemes for the unemployed.

The Community Centre opened its doors in 1980 and was officially opened by Doug Scott, the mountaineer. Maria Dabrowska was first Manager of the Crescent Community Centre and lived above, in one of two flats on the second floor. The Centre provided a drop-in point, offered refreshments, courses and events for local people who included Family First tenants. Making parents feel welcome was a priority. Next door to Family First's hostel for teenagers newly out of 'care', the Crescent Community Centre was used for their group meetings. It was also home of the Sociable Theatre, a community arts group, partly funded by the Gulbenkian Foundation. Started by local actors Bob and Sue Heskett, the Sociable Theatre took theatre to the streets, and to many groups including the children attending The Croft Family Centre day nursery and their parents.

In its early years, the Crescent Community Centre was much helped by trainees, often those in one of Family First's own training schemes funded by the Manpower Services Commission. The staff were dedicated and flexible. During a period of short-term financial crisis (1984), with stalwart determination two staff managed to keep the drop-in facilities open and the coffee bar running.

When Care in the Community was introduced and the large psychiatric hospitals started to discharge their patients, the Crescent Community Centre offered many of them newly living in the NG7 area a quality daytime and evening drop-in point. In 1986, Family First's Director Angus Walker said the Centre for several years had provided local ex-psychiatric patients who did not attend hospital day centres with:-

- A social venue when other resources were closed, particularly in the evenings and at weekends.
- A venue that was also open to other users and which helped to break

down some of the social barriers that can separate 'mentally ill' and 'normal' people.
- An opportunity for a fuller and more rewarding life through having control and choice.

Carol Stretton, Manager of the Centre for many years, said 55-60 people used the Centre daily at that time. Over the years, the number grew considerably.

One of the best loved services was the coffee bar. Hot snacks were available for much of the day and a weekly lunch club was popular. There was a pool room; a games area (including many board games); a match play dart board, and space for comfortable sitting listening to music or reading (with a large choice of books available). Outings were arranged frequently. On weekday mornings on the first floor, a community shop opened, offering good quality clothing, bric-a-brac and small household items at a non-profit making cost. A laundry was available, including on some evenings.

The Crescent Community Centre was increasingly used by local people who had been in long-stay psychiatric hospitals, in particular Mapperley Hospital on Porchester Road. The contradictions in the Government's Care in the Community Policy first became sharply visible in 1987 (see below).

At the time of Family First's 25th anniversary (1990), a report stated: ***"The catchment area of the Crescent Community Centre is one of the most socio-economically deprived ones in Nottingham and a large number of people have mental health problems . . . We see our members*** [i.e. regulars] ***as local residents of the area and not just as clients of our service. We offer informal day and evening care for individuals who may or may not be associated with statutory day care provision. Our clients consist of mainly middle-aged and elderly people with a long history of mental health disorders and who have spent long periods in a hospital setting resulting in being institutionalised. They have a large role in the day-to-day running of the services at the Centre, have their own members' Management Committee and meet once a month to discuss activities, outings, new member allocations and any issues they raise."***

Although the Crescent Community Centre was officially recognised as valuable, its staff nevertheless reported in 1990: ***"The Centre seems to be under continual threat of closure, which seems quite remarkable in view of its popularity, the high subject profile of 'community care' and the history of its development. One of the questions asked at a public meeting in January 1990 was: Where will I go if the project closes?"***

Facing closure of the Crescent Community Centre because joint revenue funding from the Health Authority and Nottingham City Social Services expired, Family First joined forces with the All Saints' Centre (Raleigh Street), a complementary service, in a public campaign. Many users of both centres were, or had been, mentally ill and lived close by, often in group homes. Attendance at the centres was voluntary and no other services were available if they closed. A public meeting chaired by Councillor Colin Bromfield and with support of the *Nottingham Evening Post* helped to secure funding for another year and redundancy notices for staff happily were withdrawn.

In 1991, Nottingham Health Authority was approached by its Forum of Voluntary Sector Representatives about the question of joint funding. Rosemary Renouf and Janice Knight said: ***"The drop-in centres provide choice for the users, are value for money, and are an integral part of community care that we must defend."***

The Community Support Unit of Nottinghamshire County Council in 1991/92 prepared a report for its senior management team on joint financed voluntary sector mental health projects because joint funding (Social Services/Health Authority) was due to end in 1992. Two out of four of the projects were run by Family First: The Crescent Community Centre and Miscellany (see below). The report stated: ***"The Crescent Community Centre is largely used by people living in registered homes in the local area, who were formerly long-stay patients in a psychiatric hospital. There are over 100 people in contact with the Centre, 90% of whom are known to the statutory mental health services. Most people who attend are aged over fifty (75%), and male (90%).***

"The Centre is open four-and-a-half days a week, plus three evenings including Sundays, with lunches provided on four days. The project also runs a coffee bar, a clothes shop with good second-hand clothes and has washing machines. Trips out are organised on a fairly regular basis. There are close links with the Health Authority. The facilities are also used by the Mental Health Unit staff and patients three days a week."

Despite the problems of funding, the staff team at the Crescent Community Centre continued to do their very best, realising that if the Centre did not exist, many people's lives would be, at best, more isolated and, at worst, deeply unhappy.

Family First Management Committee member Clyde Moore, a policeman, agreed to have his head shaved (1993) and thus raised money towards a holiday for some of the Centre members. Centre staff worked hard year after year to find organisations to sponsor members' outings. For example, members visited Meadow Lane several times to watch Notts County, for some a first experience of going to a football match; museums, and Stonebridge City Farm. They went on a mystery trip and one to the coast, and joined in Chinese New Year and Diwali celebrations.

An especially thoughtful offer came from Nottingham Castle Museum staff who volunteered 'memory lane' sessions. They showed and discussed items and artefacts from the past. This special link with Nottingham Castle Museum staff provided Centre members with opportunity to learn more about local heritage and culture, culminating in a spectacular party at Newstead Abbey with members and staff wearing period costume.

Members organised social events at the Centre, welcoming all in the area, for example, a bonfire night firework display, plus pie and peas. It was a thriving community centre, and was a very popular choice for trainee and social work student placements.

Carol Stretton, Manager, who made sure the Crescent Community Centre was 'for everybody', said in 1994: ***"We look to the future with a degree of uncertainty because of anticipated reduction in Social Services grant aid budget. However, we will continue with our endeavours to help teach social and life skills, dismantle prejudices and hopefully try to improve the quality of life for our members."*** Both Carol Stretton, and 'the coffee bar lady', made a huge difference to many people's lives: they are well-remembered and inspired students with ideas to take into their futures.

Two stairlifts were installed (1995) in the Crescent Community Centre with a Nottinghamshire County Council mental illness specific grant. They provided access to the whole building. The Centre had to close during the evenings because of a funding shortfall. In 1996, improvements included internal and external decorating and an improved craft room. A mental health specific grant supported the cost of furniture for a smoke-free quiet room. Efforts to increase funding included a renewed drive to hire out rooms. New users were Local Authority Housing Training Services, and medical surgeries run from the Centre for men and women experiencing 'combat stress' (i.e. ex-war veterans).

An example of how a neighbourhood centre can transform lives is provided by a member, AP who (1996) was able to go to the Employment Office to say he would be working [i.e. earning] to cover for a staff member for three months and would not need benefit. ***"I enjoyed helping the members and assisting with the dinners. I also assisted with playing Bingo which I liked. I got to know everybody and helping them do things made me feel good. We took some members on a trip to the [Sneinton] Windmill where we all made bread which was great. I enjoyed the whole experience and it has given me more confidence to look for a job."*** AP.

There are still many people aged over 55 who were institutionalised, sometimes for decades, before the large psychiatric hospitals closed[3]. Now that they live 'in the community' they deserve consistent opportunity to develop life skills and – above all – to feel safe among people they

[3] Mapperley [Psychiatric] Hospital on Porchester Road, Nottingham, closed at the end of 1994. Its patients and ex-patients were often linked to Family First services

know well and respect. They are not mere short-term 'units of expenditure'. Family First's work with people with mental health issues has had to change, but it remains constant as a practical concern.

The Crescent Community Centre at 34, Waterloo Road, had to close in July 1998. Some of its members transferred to Amity on Mansfield Road (see below). There was a plan to reopen The Crescent Community Centre in autumn 1999 with a new remit of mental health support for young black people, but this project went to other premises before moving into the first floor of Amity's premises.

The whole building at 34, Waterloo Road has now been converted into flats by Family First with funds accumulated through property disposal. There are six flats: one is for social housing. The other five are for commercial rent. Four have one bedroom and one has two-bedrooms. The commercial rent will assist the budget for improving Family First's tenanted properties.

Miscellany (later Mental Health Resource Centre)

848, Woodborough Road, Mapperley

Family First's involvement with mental health 'problems' began in the 1970s. At the back of Miscellany, Family First's first owned shop (1971) in Mapperley, was a workroom used by volunteers to sort, iron and pack clothes. It was also a rest room for shop volunteers.

These back premises soon developed into an informal mini-community centre. It proved to be a space in which people who were often isolated felt comfortable, not least because they were accepted as equals and not treated as 'clients' or 'patients'. They enjoyed sharing time and, also, purposeful activity. The focus for the activity was, in fact, the shop which was run in a professional way. Some volunteers, for example, helped to make sheets for cots and prams: they were made from the good parts of flannelette sheets which were cut out and stitched. Unravelling the good wool from old knitted garments was a useful skill: knitting and crocheting the washed good wool for new uses was another. There were many low income families who benefited from items that were useful, low cost and had been made with love by volunteers.

For several years, I had been a regular visitor to nearby Mapperley (Psychiatric) Hospital on Porchester Road to visit Family First tenants (including young women living at Mayholme/The Croft) or others in touch with Family First who were in the hospital. It became evident that, for some patients, there was need for a pop-in place nearby which they could visit in the daytime. It was agreed that qualified hospital staff might suggest to suitable patients that they could pop in to the back of nearby Miscellany and join in daytime activities. The number of people who popped in grew.

In 1976, the back of Miscellany extended and became a proper workshop where activities would be structured to an extent but the atmosphere still informal. Ann Shorrock, who started as a volunteer, was employed to look after the project. At the time I wrote:***"this is yet another illustration of how much easier it is to assist people when there is a practical reason for them being somewhere."***

In 1987, with their permission, Miscellany staff gathered life stories from some of the users in order to explain how Miscellany 'worked'. Here are three of the stories:-

* ***"Harry's mother remarried when he was 10. His stepfather was always bullying him and putting him down. Eventually, he went on hunger strike and was referred to St Ann's Children's Hospital. It was at an early age, therefore, that his damaging experiences of bullying authority and psychiatry began. Harry's attitude to authority – imposed on him by hospital and registered home regimes – is simultaneously rebellious and deferential. He is full of criticism but finds it impossible to challenge directly . . . At Miscellany workshop he seems free from nagging, constant criticisms and put-downs and can relax, joke, entertain and support others.***

It is remarkable to see how quickly he reverts into the role of patient when anybody labelled 'social worker' or 'nurse' visits. We

feel it is a tribute to the environment that he can relate to and communicate with us, beyond our roles. Life at the registered home where he now lives is experienced by Harry as demeaning, regimented by mealtimes, bedtimes and chucking-out times. He will probably spend the rest of his life there. Miscellany seems the only place where he is genuinely recognised and appreciated as an individual."

* *"John is married and has two children. He worked as a joiner for 16 years. A nervous breakdown caused him to retire from work. Miscellany workshop offers John pride and self-esteem, as well as company. John attends classes to enable him to make even more of a practical contribution to the workshop. He prefers to operate in an environment that does not carry pressure or stigma, and to work at a level he chooses. Miscellany sometimes provides John with a forum to explore and discuss political and current issues which he finds stimulating."*

* *"Carole was an intelligent, 'liberated' mother of four, who at one time worked in the Probation Service. Three years ago, her ex-husband abducted her two youngest children abroad. A breakdown followed. She spent months sleeping rough and in night shelters, in a state of unreality and confusion. In Nottingham, she was admitted to Mapperley Hospital, and then spent a year in a registered home. During this time, Miscellany workshop was her lifeline. She attended every day. It seemed to provide an environment that was neither damaging nor patronising. It gave her a sense of purpose to fight the numbing lethargic haze of tranquilisation and space to grow in strength and confidence to the time when she was ready to move on. We still maintain contact, and sometimes offer support. Carole is now living in her own house, independently."*

Over time, the drop-in centre at the back took on the name Miscellany and the shop lost it, though the shop is still there, selling furniture now.

By the time Family First was 25 years old, the national policy of Care in the Community was having an impact on Miscellany as it had with the Crescent Community Centre. In 1990, Miscellany staff reported: *"During the year a number of people have been moved out of Mapperley (and other psychiatric hospitals) and into the local community. There is an increase in the number of users with housing problems and/or staying unsupported in local hostels. Miscellany is strongly needed to offer support and a place to go.*

"The preventive nature of our work is important. Several people who use the project gain support at a critical time in their lives and do not become reliant on the statutory services. We cannot quantify this aspect of our work; nevertheless it is crucial to our assessment of the success of the project."

The 1991/92 report of Nottinghamshire County Council's Community Support Unit described Miscellany as: *"A small day centre on the Woodborough Road [Mapperley]. It opens 9-5 each day except Thursday. There is a leaning towards creative, artistic activities. There is a second-hand clothes store and a food co-operative. Emphasis is placed on the project being run and owned by the users.*

"Miscellany is in contact with 50-60 people, with 15-20 using the project each day. No records of individuals are kept, but almost all have had in-patient periods in psychiatric hospital and most are still in touch with mental health services. There is a wide age range of users, attracting more young people than Family First's Crescent Community Centre and the All Saints' Community Centre. Effort is made to respond to the needs of women and a women-only session is held on one morning. There is a small but increasing number of black users."

Miscellany had craft and workshop facilities, with support, and offered a wide range of activities including clay modelling, glass painting, T-shirt painting and various types of drawing. There were shared meals including cooking, and outings. Aromatherapy was on offer. The role of Miscellany had always been viewed as preventative as well as rehabilitative.

Staff stressed (1993): *"As more people are being moved out of Mapperley Hospital and into the local community (e.g. Alexandra*

Court, Macmillan Court, bed and breakfasts), projects such as Miscellany will be needed to offer services which can empower people who are used to an institutional framework." Attendance grew steadily and included many young people. In 1995, in conjunction with Nottingham Ecoworks, woodworking and gardening were added to available activities.

In 1996, in collaboration with Nottingham Advocacy Group[4], Miscellany established a user forum as a way forward to a user-led service. A laundry facility was added to the range of existing services. By 1997, Miscellany was called a social centre and included information technology training with grant aid from Nottinghamshire County Council and the mental health charity MIND, and use was made of the training opportunities available in Family First's Furniture and Clothing Service.

"Thank you for supporting us like no-one else could have, these last two years have been among the most positive of my life." Member (1997).

Statutory politics exerts its power – again

Family First Management Committee in December 1987 was given a report that there were policy changes imminent concerning Health Authority joint funding for Family First's mental health support at Crescent Community Centre and Miscellany. The Revd Paul Watts [then Director of Nottingham Council for Voluntary Service] said: ***"The application for the Crescent Community Centre is being scrutinised because it does not deal exclusively with mental health users, but to change our way of working would be unacceptable to Family First."*** In other words, it would be unfair to isolate mental health users who in Family First's neighbourhood projects were genuinely 'in the community'.

In 1991/92 the statutory agency report (already referred to) stated that the Crescent Community Centre and Miscellany projects, the All Saints' Community Centre and MIND volunteer project were: ***"valuable community services. The more informal nature of the day care projects, as opposed to the more structured statutory mental health day centres, increases the variety and choice available to users. The Crescent Community Centre and the All Saints' projects meet a particular need for day care users in the Nottingham NG7 district, where most of the registered homes (mental health) are situated. Miscellany offers a more therapeutically orientated service, emphasising user empowerment".***

But times and policies were changing. The evolving rationale for funding mental health projects seemed to disregard aspects of 'in the community'. Funding became more difficult. There were complex reasons for the ending of sound projects that really worked for people who needed them. What were the reasons? They included the changes brought about by Nottingham City Council becoming a Unitary Authority; the politics of Care in the Community agendas within the mental health statutory sector; the developing culture of 'best value' that assumed a tick-box rather than a human face, and the responsibility of the Family First Board, a Board motivated and well-qualified but perhaps at that time with too little day-to-day understanding of the issues and the politics enveloping them.

From the archives of 1997, it is clear that decisions surrounding the future of Family First's mental health services were fraught. Funding for these services was being squeezed (as a way of forcing decision-making?). A member of the Family First Board was also involved professionally, as Directorate Manager RCCS [Nottingham – NHS - Rehabilitation and Community Care Services]. He put forward the proposal that Family First should take over the NHS-run mental health centre at 702, Mansfield Road and that a service could be maintained there for those individuals with mental health issues who used Family First's Miscellany and Crescent Community Centre.

Family First's Director, Graham Wright wrote to Carol Stretton, experienced Manager of the Crescent Community Centre, stating that the NHS professional panel had not been a steering group looking at Family First Services but one that would

[4] The Nottingham Advocacy Group, established in 1985, promotes the interests of users and ex-users of the psychiatric services. It is still based in the Miscellany building

decide whether 702 Mansfield Road should transfer to Family First. However, a Family First proposal did contain a detailed outline of the future of the Crescent Community Centre and Miscellany, in relation to 702, Mansfield Road although it was admitted that 'time constraints have prevented proper consultation'. If 702, Mansfield Road were transferred to Family First to use, it would not own the building [in other words it could be sold over Family First's head unlike both the Crescent Community Centre and Miscellany which it owned].

Many Crescent Community Centre and Miscellany Staff were unhappy at these projects losing their individual identity because both, with their very different roles were fully used, much needed and inclusive. But a management strait-jacket was the outcome of a proposal, which looked to the inexperienced as if it met all the latest criteria, being made and agreed.

What about the users of 702, Mansfield Road, and those of Miscellany and the Crescent Community Centre that had to close soon after? In the lead-up to the changes in Family First's mental health services there was some marked difference of views on the part of managers (both NHS and Family First) between those who saw damage to users in the changes and those who wanted to work out 'new projects' from a theoretical perspective. There was a lot of distress and much genuine concern on both sides.

NHS staff at 702, Mansfield Road, believed the NHS Manager, who was also a Family First Board member, had 'something against' their centre as he had tried to close it in 1996. They were deeply unhappy at proposed changes and wrote protesting to the Chief Executive, Nottingham Healthcare NHS Trust.

The name Miscellany was dropped in 1998 and the back premises and upstairs of its premises at 848, Woodborough Road became the Mental Health Resource Centre. The younger people who had used Miscellany tended to 'disappear' as its drop-in place and arts/crafts workshops ended.

In 1999, the Mental Health Resource Centre was relaunched in order to co-ordinate and develop counselling services and volunteering projects as well as mental health support groups. The Centre established counselling, natural therapy and volunteer programmes and developed a number of groups supporting people experiencing mental health difficulties. For the next few years, this Centre was used primarily for groups run by tutors, volunteers and staff members for participants from city and county and for counselling sessions for individuals. By 2004, it was not being used by Family First. It continues to be used by the Nottingham Advocacy Group.

Amity, 702, Mansfield Road, Nottingham

> ***"Mental ill-health affects one in six members of the population at any one time in their lives."*** Department of Health. 1999. This is a salutary point to remember.

From December 1997, Family First took over 702, Mansfield Road as a day centre named Amity. The building was owned by the NHS and had been used as a Nottingham Health Care NHS Trust Mental Health Centre.

In 1998, Amity attracted some of the members in the older age groups who previously used the Crescent Community Centre or 702, Mansfield Road NHS project. Within 16 months, Amity had increased services to include literacy and information technology. It had 97 users registered as members with an average daily attendance of 21, far fewer than had attended the Crescent Community Centre and Miscellany. But, as always, Family First's 'staff on the job' were and are committed to creating opportunity and providing a welcoming daytime place for people who live in registered homes and/or who have few family links.

Members at Amity have mental health support needs but may, or may not, be using statutory mental health services. The aim at Amity is to develop self-awareness and self-esteem, communication and independent living skills, to help members to gain awareness of health/mental health needs and to develop strategies to manage them. Many of the members live in registered residential homes (e.g. with 14 bedrooms). Some move on into supported housing (e.g. houses for three or four people). ***"They [the commissioning NHS body] have started putting 20/22-year-olds into residential homes,"*** Paul Hudson, Project Team Leader, told me (2004). ***"It is not appropriate for them. They should be in supported housing."***

When new members start with Amity, they are asked to choose one group to join in order to begin to build up a structure to their lives. There are 12 groups on offer, including music; IT drop-in; Members' Committee; shared learning (often about local reminiscing); photography; ethics; arts and crafts; lunch club once a week, and relaxation. There is personal support and advice. In 2004, 16 new people chose to start at Amity (11 men and 5 women) ***"This place is run by the members not us, it's their choice what groups they have,"*** said Paul Hudson. Members take part in outreach work, including public exhibitions of their work, some of which is sold.

"I think the word 'mental' is a stigma," Paul Hudson says. ***"Everyone has a problem somewhere in their life but mention someone's got a mental problem and it's: 'they're crackers'."*** Paul Hudson first went to Amity as a trainee from a training agency after being made redundant from Raleigh. Following the training period, he returned as a volunteer. He then became a part-time support worker which increased to full time. In 2003, he became Project Team Leader.

Amity has become a valuable project for people with long experience of mental health establishments. They can express their individuality and increase their independence and skills in many ways. Members made a list of what Amity meant to them (2004). Views included: ***"Not feeling isolated and being out there alone"; "Friendship"; "Trying to get back out into the community"; "Giving support at the doctor's and reviews"; "Somewhere to go"; "Something to look forward to after the weekend"; "Wanting to get back to normality"; "Not being institutionalised"; "Learning to trust people again"; "Keeping people off the streets stops us getting into trouble"; "Nice place to come"; "Learning new skills"; "Meeting people who also hear voices and getting support"; "Knowing people care about us" and "We rely on the day centre and staff being there for us."***

Paul Hudson told me (2005) that the All Saints' project (Raleigh Street) closed in November 2005. Family First was now the only voluntary organisation provider of a mental health day centre in the city. Funding was secure until 2007. Then what? The Amity property, as we saw earlier, belongs to the NHS. So the property could realise a substantial sum to ease the local [NHS] Primary Care Trust's funding problems. One of the more tragic aspects of such closures as the All Saints' project, says Paul Hudson, is the loss of security for a group of people who do not deserve such displacement. He said: ***"It often takes a member some two to three years before they learn to trust us. We learn to understand individual needs, the treatment they are on . . . Amity has 80 members and five on the waiting list. Where will the 150 from All Saints go?"*** He dreaded to think what life would be like for members if there was nowhere secure and friendly to use during the day, where there was a range of activities, and where skills were developed.

Like other Family First projects, Amity enjoys placements of students, trainees and volunteers. It is not unusual for students or trainees to return as volunteers.

Amity is now attracting younger users and (2005) started a Young People's Group once a week. This is for young adults up to the age of 30, referred by social workers or self-referrals. Amity and Young Diverse Minds (YDM) work together in this group (see below).

Young Diverse Minds (YDM)

YDM is a mental health project for young people aged 16-25 from Afro-Caribbean, Asian and dual heritage backgrounds. A project paper explains that help is for those ***"who are experiencing a range of emotional and psychological feelings, behaviour and symptoms, who may or may not be using statutory mental health services".*** The project, initially called Young Black Minds

(YBM), was to be situated in the Crescent Community Centre on Waterloo Road. YBM had a couple of moves and is now settled on the first floor at Amity, 702, Mansfield Road.

YBM opened in June 2000 and aimed to develop self-esteem and to assist with communication skills. Services included referral and assessment, individual support and links to counselling and complementary care. In 2001, the project received a grant from the European Social Fund.

Some months later, at members' request, the project name changed to Young Diverse Minds (YDM). Outreach is a key part of this project and 90 young people were contacted in 2003: 11 were helped on a one-to-one basis, along with information about medication, housing and benefits. There was access to complementary therapies and independent advocacy.

"I like the company and having an opportunity to chat. I hope you will see me again." Member (2003).

In 2004, 80 new contacts were made by phone, face to face or by letter. Substantial work was achieved with 15 young people. The project also assists people to access other appropriate organisations, e.g. housing services, immigration advice and educational advancement.

Since sharing premises with Amity, members in this project have the opportunity to do art work, digital photography and music. Much work is one-to-one suited to individual mental health needs.

Sally Simnett, Project Team Leader, says YDM is funded by the Primary Care Trust and the Health Care Trust. ***"People hear of us through word of mouth, faith groups, community psychiatric nurses, or maybe a family member will have heard of us or seen some information. They will ring us up and ask us to come in and talk with some brother, daughter . . . The biggest barrier we face is the fact that, because we are working with young people, there's this label of mental health and they don't want to know. Mental health problem: me? No!"***

"Some people want to sit and talk and they want someone to listen to them, some want to be more active in the community. For instance, they want confidence built up, like being able to get on a bus again . . . little things we do at the beginning can really act as a stepping stone . . . We have seen people now being able to go to college."

Several participants in YDM have said they would like to meet other young people so ideas are being explored for a young persons' group. Sally Simnett (2005) told me: ***"We are meeting the funders next week and we hope they are going to say 'yes, you can go ahead and do that and you are not breaking any of the rules'. Even if it's only five or six people coming along, that's five or six meeting other young people."***

Sally Simnett believes the work within YDM is valuable. ***"It is breaking down barriers and challenging the stereotypical image of what a young black man is . . . drugs, guns, irresponsible, won't work, lazy: all of that which is <u>not</u> true."***

"After six months of regular support, advice and counselling, C is now showing signs of willingness to engage with the public, taking an active part in weekly activity and is expressing his own view concerning what he wishes to do . . . He was referred to Young Diverse Minds by his Community Psychiatric Nurse (CPN). When he joined, he was very fearful." Staff member (2005).

In 2005, a mixed social group started one afternoon a week at Amity because some of the young people wanted to meet each other. Some YDM members also wanted their own women-only swimming group and a men's activity group.

Another joint initiative between Amity and YDM is an advocacy group at the NHS Child and Adolescent Mental Health Unit at Thorneywood, Nottingham. A team member from each of the Family First projects runs the group once a month. These initiatives are carried out on existing funding. Both Sally Simnett and Paul Hudson (Amity) work far longer hours than those for which they are paid. They and their staff/volunteers deserve to be allowed to continue to build these creative projects. And, most importantly, members deserve continuity.

Lunch-time at Family First's Crescent Community Centre (1980-1998). Despite the photo-fault blur, this shows the pleasant tree-lined green space between Waterloo Road and Waterloo Crescent. See chapter on Neighbourhood Centres

From 1971, the volunteers' room behind the Miscellany shop in Mapperley was increasingly used by people who popped in for company and useful activity. The space was modernised and extended as a pop-in workshop in 1976. Later it was called a day centre (seen here) and used increasingly by people with mental health issues. It offered activities including diverse crafts until 1997/98. See chapter on Neighbourhood Centres

At Amity, Family First's day centre for people with mental health issues (1997). Amity is much liked by members who hope it will not be axed due to funding politics outside Family First's control. See chapter on Neighbourhood Centres

One of Family First's vans used for collecting and delivering furniture. Family First's named furniture vans have been seen in and around Nottingham since late 1966 and have helped to make its recycling services well known

Laundry

Family First opened a laundry at Highcross Court, Clifford Street, Radford, NG7, on April 10th, 1989. From the archives, it appears that the premises were offered to Family First to rent and it was decided to run a laundry service for the elderly and for residents with disabilities in Nottingham. It was not setting out to compete with other laundries or launderettes.

Despite the enthusiasm of staff and volunteers, and offering a real and appreciated service to those using it, the laundry was finding it hard to be sustainable. In 1990/91, with only three staff, there were technical problems with the equipment. Contracts for Help the Homeless and other hostel accommodation were made. Staff, helped by trainees and dedicated volunteers, dealt with 4,828 washes spread over 646 regular users. The laundry offered a sheltered workshop environment for youngsters taking their first steps towards employment.

There was a client list of 825 by 1992, and a 24-hour turn-round of laundry belonging to frail, elderly, housebound and physically disabled people, plus the contracts for Nottingham Help the Homeless at its Canal Street shelter and the Macedon Trust at the Albion Centre, Sneinton. But it was reported that ***"Running the service has again been a struggle for survival."***

It would be good to report that the laundry lasted. It started because premises were offered and a good idea was born. But it was not well thought through and, alas, the laundry closed. Whether it might have succeeded with modern equipment in more suitable premises and with a realistic three-year business plan, there is no means of knowing now.

Nottingham's Family First 1965-2005 ISBN 09550948 01

RECYCLING

For all of its 40 years, Family First has been recycling. Its Furniture and Clothing Service developed quickly. In later years the terms furniture service, shops and – more recently – recycling have been used. By 1968, Family First's Furniture and Clothing Service was recognised as Nottingham city's official service. It has grown to meet continuing and new needs, added Kidstuff and the white goods recycling workshop. Family First's vans are a familiar sight as they criss-cross the city and its environs. Over four decades, thousands of people have donated their still-good furniture, household goods and clothing. Today, there is serious political debate about conserving energy, preventing indiscriminate waste and a need to prevent profligate dumping in infill sites. Recycling is an essential contribution towards a more sustainable future. Family First has been in this respect, as others, a pioneer, although the term 'recycling' was seldom used in the early years.

Furniture and Clothing Service

As soon as Family First started, there was urgent need for furniture and clothing to help many families and individuals. It was as if the city had been waiting for this service to happen! For some months, it was an extraordinary voluntary effort. Sometimes, Family First would appeal for specific items to meet, say, an urgent request from the Probation Department about a family with no bedding. Larger items were taken by volunteers directly from donors to families in need. There was no Family First van for some months. Proper organisation of the Service evolved speedily.

In the mid-1960s, many inner-city areas of Nottingham were, or were about to be, in turmoil due to massive redevelopment programmes, including Radford, St Ann's, and the Meadows. New estates were built or about to be built. Many thousands of people were compulsorily displaced. Associated with redevelopment were years of planning blight: of streets with houses emptied of their inhabitants but into which the Council temporarily often placed homeless families. Other streets were boarded up or half pulled down, with broken lighting and rubbish accumulating for weeks, sometimes months, before proper demolition started. It is important to understand this background. The quick growth of the Furniture and Clothing Service was a direct response to hardships that families were suffering.

An early example of need was described by a woman who wrote to the *Nottingham Evening Post* on November 7th, 1966, stating that she was thrown out of her home by her husband, even though she had helped to purchase the house and furniture. She was able only to take her baby son. An estate agent found her a flat and, ***"with £10 from the Assistance Board"***, she started to rebuild her life. She obtained custody of her other four children, but she desperately needed furniture and bedding. Family First provided essential household items so the family could survive whilst it found ways to thrive, and thrive it did. She wrote: ***"There must be many children in Nottingham today who have warm clothing and comfy beds because Family First cares enough to help others to whom life has been unkind."***

Prior to Family First's Furniture and Clothing Service, social workers searched for household items and clothing for their clients, often buying them at disproportionate cost in order to 'solve a problem'. This also cost professional time (= money).

Soon, the Furniture Service was furnishing houses and flats Family First rehabilitated in order to create homes for fair rent. Tenants often arrived with only the possessions they could carry in cases, boxes or plastic bags.

Family First put regular small advertisements in the *Nottingham Evening Post* asking for still-good clothing, household goods and furniture. The Press was supportive with articles. Social workers, health visitors and hospital social workers increased requests for help for their clients: for example, a commode for an elderly person, a bed-settee for someone who needed to sleep downstairs, a pram for a struggling mother with a baby, a houseful of furniture for someone 'burned out' the previous night.

In July1967, Family First wrote to the Local Authority with details of the volume of referrals to the Furniture and Clothing Service in excess of its own requirements for furnishing properties. The Local Authority offered to help to find a suitable warehouse for Family First to rent. But nothing materialised. Family First found a suitable building in Bentinck Road, Radford, that could be converted into flats and which had a large warehouse behind. The Local Authority refused a mortgage application for £5,000. The Town Clerk said: ***"In reaching this decision, the Committee were, of course, aware and appreciative of the good work which is carried out by Family First and the Committee are anxious to help whenever they can."*** The Estates Surveyor was instructed to find alternative suitable premises. Nothing happened, except that referrals for help from the Furniture and Clothing Service grew.

In March 1968, the Nottingham Council of Social Service called a meeting of the city's main organisations, statutory and voluntary, which had an interest in a furniture service. As a result, Family First was formally appointed as agent for a city-wide scheme. The various bodies said they would chip in with starter finance but only £10 came from the Rotary Club!

Family First met referrals from city agencies, including Social Services, Probation Department, hospital social workers and the Department of Health and Social Security [DHSS]. With hindsight, it is clear Family First was running a community business (or social enterprise) long before that concept was recognised. At that time, costs of running the service were met through (a) DHSS[1] payments against invoices per referral for items needed; (b) funds Family First raised by selling clothing and household goods at very low cost direct to families/individuals in need, and (c) fund-raising to cover expenses for goods for which nothing could be charged.

Family First's small bright yellow van was on the road six or seven days a week and was insufficient transport. John Player and Son gifted a 35cwt Bedford van in 1968. On occasions, I would drive the van to learn first hand about donors and recipients, storage and administrative needs.

For around 10 years, much of the loading/delivery work of the furniture van/s was done by off-duty firemen topping up their income to a satisfactory level. They were reliable, safe drivers and good with people. The van teams also dismantled furniture and put it together again when delivering to elderly people or those with disabilities. The firemen enjoyed the work, not only for the then needed extra earnings, but because it was relaxing for them to meet the public 'in normal circumstances'.

For example, one morning a fireman arrived after cutting a driver out of a crashed train engine. The advisability of him working after such a traumatic experience was discussed. Shouldn't he go home and sleep? He said the house would be empty just then and ***"you don't sleep straight after something like that. You need to do something normal and not be alone".*** I mention this only as an example of how needs are multi-faceted.

Another approach to the Local Authority (1970) produced no help. A national charity donated £2,000 towards the cost of a small dry garage/warehouse at the back of the house Family First purchased at 846, Woodborough Road, next to one of its shops, Miscellany.

In 1973, Social Services asked for details of the furniture supplied to people referred to the Furniture Service. In just six months, 219 applicants referred mainly by social workers had been helped with a total of 473 items, including 151 beds. This did not include smaller items that went into the shops, nor did it include furniture supplied to Family First properties or to people from whom no payment was possible

[1] The Assistance Board was replaced by the DHSS in 1968. In 1988, the Department split into the Department of Health and the Department of Social Security [DSS]. One of the DSS's subdivisions is the Benefits Agency launched in 1991

The garage/warehouse was insufficient and for years Family First rented a number of additional spaces. City Council help in either renting, or lending funds to purchase, a proper warehouse never materialised. In April 1976, with a bank overdraft and monies from two properties sold because they were no longer suitable, a warehouse for the Furniture Service and adjoining workshop for Family First's housing maintenance work was acquired at Kilbourn Street, off Huntingdon Street (where, with added adjoining properties, it still resides). Demands on the Furniture and Clothing Service continued to grow.

In 1982, Family First purchased 375, Alfred Street North, next to its warehouse on Kilbourn Street. The premises were extensively improved and extended by Family First supervisors/trainees. I was asked to open the premises on May 25th, 1983. They included a new shop, more warehouse space and some office space.

In 1996/97, a property at 8, Kilbourn Street was purchased. It had a single-storey workshop with storage space and offices. Around the same time, a plot of land was purchased, thus linking Family First's new purchase to its existing premises on Kilbourn Street and 375, Alfred Street North. The plot between the two built areas became a van and car park for Family First.

Until 1988, Family First's trainees helped in the Furniture Service. After 1988, trainees from training agencies (including Family First's ex-training division) did placements with the Furniture Service, as until the 1990s did offenders ordered by a court to do a specified number of hours of Community Service. Volunteers have also always been involved.

In the UK in 1988, 36% of the adult workforce was low paid (less than £123 per week); 65% of single parents were below the poverty line, and 27% of all childless people below pension age were in poverty. Over 3m people were unemployed. Figures stated at a conference of the National Federation of Housing Associations, July 4th and 5th, 1988.

The Furniture Service is one of the largest in the UK. Many people, and some organisations, tend to think that anyone can run a comprehensive furniture service. They say: ***"Isn't it just a matter of people giving you what they don't want and then you give it to people who need it?"*** It is not! For example, one week many social agencies will make urgent requests for beds when lots of donors have decided they will donate their good second-hand dining tables!

There is skill in drawing up collection and delivery schedules to economise time and petrol; warehousing; stock control; dealing with referral agencies; organising the van fleet and drivers/mates; disposing of unusable items in the most environmentally friendly way; making sure the Furniture Service is financially underpinned, and there are always emergencies. The Furniture Service, to be well run, is a very complex operation which, as well as helping many people, saves the public purse huge expense year after year. There is skill in communicating with the public, including about standards. As Patrick Taylor, Family First's Director of Community Resources and Support Services, told me (2003): ***"If furniture is of a standard that we would not be prepared to use ourselves, we cannot send it out."***

In 1990/91, the Furniture Service had 1,907 referrals compared with 1,356 the previous year. The increase was partly because the DSS, following Government policy, for a while offered more loans than grants for necessary furniture. Also, unemployment and the then depressed economic climate created more needs. Family First continued to help people on low income but ineligible for referrals. At this time, the Furniture and Clothing Service had 10 trainees, working as driver's mates, warehouse staff and shop assistants. Some obtained permanent jobs after their training period. Those who did not sometimes chose to stay as volunteers in preference to 'doing nothing'.

Other changes in payment methods for furniture happened in the early 1990s, under new national benefit arrangements. Essential furniture was supplied free to families referred from Social Services, Welfare Rights,

Age Concern and the Health Authority, etc. Each referral was charged £3 towards administrative costs. The main financial support for the Furniture Service came through funding by the City Council's housing budget and the County Council's Social Services budget. One-third of costs was covered by direct Family First sales and fund-raising. Payment on a grant basis potentially makes for more efficiency (less paperwork etc), but it also makes for unpredictability in forward planning when grants are suddenly reduced. It also disguises the fact that the grant is, in fact, modest payment for a necessary and efficient service and should be honoured as such.

A Family First report 1991/92 erroneously stated that, in its early days, the Furniture Service was funded by its tenants. Their Family First homes were already furnished when they moved in (see Housing chapter), but they sometimes purchased furniture from the service when they moved into unfurnished Council flats/houses.

The Furniture Service by the early 1990s had four radio controlled vehicles covering a radius of 20 miles around the city. By then (very different to the mid-1960s) there was broad acceptance that families facing emergencies or hardship should have access to household essentials. But, whilst families and individuals in need receive good quality furniture, they do not get (as critics maintain) expensive new furniture. Today (end of 2005) people can contact Family First's recycling services through one of the recognised referral agencies and are required to pay an administration fee of £10. If they are referred to Family First, they receive basic items of furniture and white goods to enable them to set up home. Parents can also be referred to Kidstuff (see below).

Throughout the years, some furniture and clothing have been for sale at modest cost from the Family First shops. Occasionally antiques have been sold at a realistic cost to assist funds.

From March 1st, 1993, under EEC regulations, it became illegal to give or sell foam-filled furniture that did not meet the new regulations. It was a necessary regulation but presented a potential short-term problem to the Furniture Service. It would take at least two or three years before accredited foam began to be donated. Via MPs and the National Furniture Recycling Network, it was agreed that pre-regulation foam stock could be used for a limited duration providing it had warning labels affixed.

The Furniture Service took over the Business Recycling Scheme from the Nottinghamshire branch of Action Resource Centre (1994). Large firms and institutions gave surplus office furniture and equipment for use by community groups and small charities. In 1995, for example, donations of equipment and business furniture were made by 80 local companies and given to over 100 local charities and community organisations. This scheme worked well and lasted for several years until supply and demand withered due to changing times.

During 1994, the Furniture Service had a short spell of inefficiency due to poor management and missing goods. Firm remedial steps were taken during Moira Cole's period as Chair of the Management Committee. After this time, Patrick Taylor joined Family First as Manager of the Furniture Service and soon had the problems licked and the service back in good shape. Family First's occasional blips have been dealt with efficiently, except when Housing Corporation pressure created internal difficulty over housing policy for a period in the 1990s. Licking that problem subsequently was not an internal option, because Family First's hands are tied by the Corporation (see Housing chapter and Appendix II).

Rushcliffe Borough Council promoted the Furniture Service through a leaflet drop in 1996 which increased donations of furniture by 15% over the year. The computerised system (set up by Terry Campbell, Service Manager of Community Resources) created a more efficient system in 1996 for recording referrals and maintaining stock control.

In 1996, after closure of the Government's Community Action Programme, trainees continued to play an important role in the Furniture Service. They came from various training agencies and under the voluntary sector option of the Government's New Deal working in partnership with Arnold & Carlton College.

Kevin West, now Warehouse Supervisor, told (1999) his experience of coming to Family First as a trainee: ***"After working 18 years at British Coal and being made redundant, along with many others, you fall into the trap of 'I'll have a rest and look for a job later'. Five years later and still having a rest I thought it was time to do something because when you start to like Richard and Judy and cooking programmes [on TV], I knew it was time to get off my backside and do something and I did – I became a trainee at Family First and gained Level 1 and 2 NVQ in warehousing and retail.***

"When I first started, it was hard to fit in because of all the other personalities but I kept on going and started to enjoy working with other trainees and the paid members of staff who were a pleasure to work with. They were kind and supportive all the time not just with me but to all the trainees, who seem to want to come back again and again. They do volunteering work or work on Government schemes. A lot of trainees find work after being at Family First or are still working for Family First. By the way, you know how I mentioned paid members of staff. Well, I'm one of those now after a year-and-a-half of hard work."

In 1997, the Furniture Service and its allied services became part of the new Community Resources Division. The varied work of the division remained an excellent opportunity for employment related training. However, the name Furniture Service lingers on. In 1997, 9,869 collections were made. There were 2,130 referrals for furniture and electrical equipment involving some 15,000 items. The Furniture Service now had six vans and, in 1998, 10,250 households donated over 29,000 items of furniture.

Referrals for furniture continued to come from some 80 agencies, but mainly from the Probation Department, City Council Housing Department, Citizens Advice Bureau, Health Authority, registered social landlords, Social Services (City and County) and family advice centres. In 1998, there were 2,404 referrals for furniture and children's clothing and equipment through Kidstuff. The following year, 2,000 deliveries were made to new clients. This proves the service was not propping up a narrow band of recipients, a criticism that people who know nothing about the Furniture and Clothing Service sometimes make.

David Hunt, when chair of Family First's Board (2003), told me: ***"An important factor in Family First's longevity – when so many businesses and organisations have faded – is the strong ethical sense of its founding aims and objectives."*** These values have, over the years been defined simply as Family First's 'ethos'. Andy Churchill, Chair of the Board between David Hunt's two terms, said in Family First's Annual Report (2001) that its work was being strengthened because the unity of the organisation ***"entwined the three strands of our work – housing, community resources and community care – more closely together. In a way we have gone back to our roots as a community based organisation".***

In 2000, the value of the furniture delivered was estimated to be in excess of £2m (first year cost equivalent). This gives some idea of the value of the Furniture Service. Evidence of its quality is that during 2001, only three complaints were received and they were resolved satisfactorily. Family First had 104 surveys returned from clients referred for furniture. Of these, 78 said they would not have been able to get the furniture any other way.

"I would like to thank Family First for your help recently with furniture, clothing, kitchenware and electrical items. It has made my daughter and I much more able to settle into our new home and start our new life. Your staff dealt with my circumstances with compassion and empathy which came as a breath of fresh air at a time when things were so grim." A referral client (2000).

Mission Statement 2001

As a recognised charity and housing provider, Family First aims to deliver innovative, efficient and effective services responding to people in need within the community. Further details about Family First on www.familyfirst.org.uk.

In the year ending March 2001, despite generating £85,000 itself, Family First had a £18,000 deficit on the Furniture Service, due to insufficient financial input from the statutory sector whose clients are referred to and benefit from the service. Transport costs and salaries are not fixed overheads: more work = more costs. A grant of £400,000 over three years from the Community Fund [Lottery] was very welcome in 2001. It was to match funding from Nottinghamshire County Council and Nottingham City Council over a similar period. The Community Fund grant enabled three new vans to be purchased. One of the older ones was given to Help the Homeless in Worksop.

The pattern of referrals in 2002 was 80% from the city and 20% from the county.

Family First identified a suitable building available on lease in Bulwell for its Furniture Service warehouse; a shop; Kidstuff; white goods workshop, and support offices/parking. Negotiations had to be abruptly stopped when the proportionate grant to the Furniture Service from Nottingham City Council was unexpectedly scaled down. So, once again, Nottingham City Council prevented a reasonable step forward for a recycling service that primarily served the city.

At what stage in the UK will partnership and loyalty between statutory and community organisations be seen as a two-way process? Much is expected of community organisations. Much should also be expected of statutory agencies to act with probity for the long-term benefit of local communities whose proven skills, cost-effective enterprises and loyalties should be respected. It is so easy to destroy sound local social enterprise. The more it is knocked down, the harder it will be to motivate communities to help themselves.

Over 40 years, Family First's recycling services have adapted not only to continue a first class service but also to involve a diverse and large number of trainees and volunteers. Often, they have benefited not only from the training but also from the experience of genuine inclusion.

A major reason why larger premises are urgently needed by the Furniture and Clothing Service is to extend its social enterprise potential to generate more income by repairing furniture, thus making more available for reuse rather than ending up in infill sites. This would also offer wider training opportunities. More damaged antique furniture which is sometimes donated could be skilfully renovated and sold for funds.

Terry Campbell, Service Manager of Community Resources, said (2004) that around 10,000 sq ft of warehousing was needed to provide for furniture renovation and for more white goods to be repaired and tested. Staff tried to be strict about what they collected because the Furniture Service was not a refuse agency. "***We have to think twice about collecting used flat-pack furniture, because – as soon as it is dismantled – it can be no use.***" Two staff drivers, Andrew Bochen and Gurcharan Kandola, have been with Family First since 1989.

The Community Fund helped again in 2003 with a grant of £214,711 to develop a Family First Furniture Service including white goods in Mansfield, a former mining town north of Nottingham. The service was established within a year with its own warehouse, staff, transport and trainees.

Good news came in 2005, with the input of £170,000 over three years from the [Lottery] Community Recycling and Economic Development Programme (CRED) to expand provision of Family First's recycling services, in particular in relation to the tonnage Family First is able to recycle through its furniture and white goods projects and shops. The funding includes paying for a Family First recycling officer Dawn Pollard early in 2006, and for a shops manager for the Mansfield area. This is a new role for Mike Toner.

Late in 2005, Family First opened a shop in the main shopping area of Sutton-in-Ashfield, near Mansfield,

Clothing and shops

The earliest regular outreach of the Clothing Service soon after Family First started was a once a month sale in Bridgeway Hall in the

Meadows district. This was organised entirely by volunteers with lead organiser, Lorna Wheatcroft. Good clothes and household items were sold at low cost. Then there were jumble sales to make use of a growing amount of clothing and other items being given to Family First. Some were unsuitable for its Clothing Service where a high standard was set. Jumble sales were popular and brought in income that helped to fund Family First's work.

One of the most useful services Family First offered was layettes for new babies. Mrs Joashi, then a Health Visitor, mentions this in the Aiming for Practical Justice chapter. Individual volunteers and some groups, including the Silverdale Community Association, concentrated their efforts on knitting and stitching, collecting good baby clothes and carefully wrapping up complete layettes which helped many a mother to feel that someone cared. Some patchwork pram rugs made from good cloth of worn clothes were works of art. Skeins of unpicked wool were washed and reknitted into new fresh looking and serviceable baby garments. Layettes included enough (then terry towelling) nappies. The reputation of Family First's layettes travelled fast and the DHSS soon paid Family First a layette cost for mothers in need known to them. We tried hard to make these layettes practical and special. It was a way of saying to a mother (who we might never meet) that she and her baby mattered.

Other support groups specialised in making warm blankets for children's beds. The ingenuity used was wonderful. In Family First's early years, poverty and hardship for many people often permeated every aspect of their lives. For example, damp, cold housing; uncertain financial help; domestic violence that was sometimes condoned by agencies; prejudice often without redress in housing and in employment. That was the dark side of a society which also had many warm, friendly neighbourhoods. These often included close three and four-generation families; welcomed incomers; operated all sorts of small-scale business and social enterprises, and shared friendship and resources.

For a while, Family First operated its rapidly developing city-wide Clothing Service (with some household goods) from a small shop and back store run by a couple in Sneinton and it then rented 165, Carlton Road. The latter is recalled (in the Housing chapter) by two former Family First tenants who lived over it.

Family First opened its first owned shop Miscellany at 848, Woodborough Road, Mapperley, in 1971. It was one of the very first smart-looking charity shops. Shops Manager Edna Sharpe, previously manager of a bridal gown shop, made sure stock was clean, good quality and well displayed. The shop did well for over 20 years and met needs in an area where many families were quietly struggling. It had close links with patients at nearby Mapperley Hospital and their families. From 1996, the shop sold only non-essential items, including furniture. The name Miscellany gradually was taken over by the drop-in centre/workshop behind the shop.

In 1972, Family First purchased its second shop Scoop, with flat above, at 116, Leslie Road, off the Forest. Scoop became a mini-neighbourhood centre and information point. From 1997, a room by the side of the shop, was used as a housing office one day a week where Family First tenants in the area paid rent; reported repairs needed; signed tenancy agreements, and dealt with other housing matters. Due to Scoop's location, people would often pop in purely to chat, pass on news, inquire about something or – occasionally – ask for help in an emergency. Many students in the area were among regular customers and had their own likes. Brenda Smalley, then Shops Supervisor, told me (2005) that she sorted things for Scoop which included items students liked in order to make their accommodation friendly and functional. For example, small bookcases, and maybe a toaster and an iron that had been safety tested in the Family First white goods workshop. Many in the district were sorry to see Scoop close on October 1st, 2004.

The third shop Odds and Ends, at 95, Ilkeston Road, was purchased in 1974 and also had its distinctive role in a diverse community. It was a busy area. Odds and Ends was popular with elders. Customers included many of large sizes and the Shops Manager, Edna Sharpe, when sorting incoming clothes, would look out for special requests, for example, when a size 26 grandmother on low income needed something smart to wear to a wedding. This shop was open for some 10 years before it was sold to the owner of the shop next door who knocked the two into one.

Brenda Smalley joined Family First in 1974 to run Odds and Ends and, now part-time Shops Coordinator (late 2005), she is the longest-serving Family First staff member. Brenda worked for 10 years at Odds and Ends; over seven at Scoop, and for 14 she has been based at the shop at Kilbourn Street. She collects clothes from donors' homes, helped by a volunteer who collects twice a week. Brenda Smalley (2004) told me: ***"I've been visiting some people for years when out collecting clothes, and have seen their children grow up. People enjoy a chat when they see you again."***

Shop staff and volunteers have been and are an important part of Family First. Often, they provide an informal neighbourhood citizens' advice service and listening ear. So whilst not being able to name all who have been volunteers, here is tribute to their long service to their communities through Family First. The shops have raised significant income which assists Family First. The income has not risen proportionately to other income/expenditure because prices in the shops could not be increased pro rata. But they still make a significant contribution to funds. In 2002, for example, the shops generated over £78,000.

A shop, Second Chance, was run in the Crescent Community Centre during the years it was open. Second Chance was popular with local people, including those who used the Centre.

The first shop at Kilbourn Street opened after Family First purchased the premises in 1976 for the Furniture Service. After the adjacent buildings were purchased, the Kilbourn Street shop moved within the complex. I met two volunteers, Joan Harris and Joan Webster, at Kilbourn Street a few years ago, sorting clothes for the shops. Years ago one of them needed Family First shops to clothe her children. She said she was now ***"Putting something back".***

Kidstuff

This project was set up in 1983 by the Assist Community Programme Agency funded by the Manpower Services Commission to provide work for long-term unemployed people. It was managed by BESTCO [Better Employment Skills Training Company]. In 1989 the Community Programme ceased. BESTCO approached Family First to see if the project could be saved.

By chance, at this time David Hunt brought some of his twin sons' outgrown toys and equipment to Kidstuff. He was told the service would be shutting at least until Family First could raise funds to finance it. David Hunt sorted out the short-term finance and thus started his long association with Family First, becoming a member of its Board and then Chair twice, the second period up until 2004. Family First sourced finance for Kidstuff from Nottinghamshire County Council and took the project over in April 1989.

In its second year with Family First, Kidstuff became an integral part of its community service provision. Children's clothes and equipment were supplied to families referred mainly by social workers and health visitors, and 1,005 clients were helped with goods to an approximate value (new) of £30,000. They paid a small administration charge (£3 in 2005). Part of Kidstuff moved to Family First's furniture warehouse on Kilbourn Street which provided opportunity for trainees to mend prams, cots and playpens, etc.

In 1991/92, the amount of children's clothes and equipment collected from donors by Kidstuff's increased, and 1,189 referrals were made to Kidstuff. The lease on Kidstuff's shop in Alfreton Road expired. The project moved to 229-231, Radford Road, Hyson Green, and this shop was opened on October 16th, 1993 by Derek Cahgill, retired Chairman of Boots Charitable Trust. This trust gave Kidstuff a Leyland Daf van with its name on as an additional advertising tool.

Referrals to Kidstuff included 61% from the Health Authority and 26% from Social Services. In 1994 the Radford Road Kidstuff shop raised just over £14,000. Two years later, all Kidstuff moved to Kilbourn Street and during the year supplied children's clothing and equipment to over 1,800 clients. This service continued to fulfil a double use: helping families who needed children's clothing free or at low cost, and saving large quantities of useful items from being thrown away.

Kidstuff has continued to collect and recycle children's clothes and equipment, been helped by volunteers and trainees and become an established part of Family First's recycling services. It has a strong team of trainees/volunteers. In the year 2004/05 it collected some 2,000 items of clothing, 350 mechanical items and 375 bags of clothing and mechanical items. Of households helped, 70% were in Nottingham city and 30% in Nottinghamshire.

White goods recycling

In its early years, Family First collected a limited number of white goods in good condition. This was mainly an activity to provide Family First tenants with equipment, and referral customers with items they needed. These white goods were checked, mended and tested. A staff member who was a qualified electrician spent sessions doing this for some years. At other times professionally qualified volunteers helped.

When premises were added to Family First's site on Kilbourn Street (1997), they included a white goods workshop and a training room. In 2000, white goods recycling developed and aimed to recycle 500 items a year. This target was exceeded in 2001 with white goods being recycled both to clients on referral and for sale in Family First shops.

Ernie George, White Goods Workshop Supervisor, has worked for Family First since 1996 and been responsible with his team (including trainees) for developing its potential. Nottingham City Council gave funding of £11,000 over three years to enable the service to develop. In 2002, more than 1,200 items were recycled, including washing machines, cookers, freezers and fridges. Items are repaired if necessary, and tested for efficiency and safety. Testing all cycles on each washing machine takes a long time. To save water and money, Family First is introducing a system using recycled water. White goods recycling started in Mansfield in 2003/2004 when Family First opened a local furniture warehouse in the town.

Foreseeable future

There will be three main strands to Family First's recycling work, two traditional and one developing fast:-

1, Families experiencing difficulties and referred to Family First by recognised statutory/voluntary agencies, will continue to need back-up with household furniture, white goods and clothing.
2. Low-income families/individuals not qualifying for referral will continue to have access to Family First's services.
3. The relationship between the need to recycle more goods for environmental reasons and the need for debt reduction/avoidance among families caught up in over-spending could develop creatively. Furnishing homes with recycled items could become regarded as trendy. It could even become a preferred choice, a design challenge, for the comfortably off.

Two of Family First's shops: Miscellany in Mapperley (1971-) and Scoop (1972–2004) on Leslie Road, off the Forest, which also served as a neighbourhood meeting point for many years

After running a city-wide Furniture Service from small inadequate storage spaces for many years, Family First managed to purchase properties and land on Alfred Street North and Kilbourn Street. This is one of the central aisles in the furniture store (1983) which is currently too small to cope with the scale of work now undertaken. See Recycling chapter

Nottingham's Family First 1965-2005 ISBN 09550948 01

TRAINING AND TRAINEES, STUDENTS AND VOLUNTEERS . . .

Informal and formal training has always been a high priority within Family First: for staff; volunteers; students; trainees on assignment to Family First, and tenants and service users. When unemployment was high, a skills training division developed within Family First. This chapter offers a flavour of the flexible training opportunities offered within Family First and the integrated role that trainees, students and volunteers play.

Much has depended on volunteers. For example, volunteers were trained to form a Speakers' Group soon after Family First started. They visited organisations, schools and associations that enquired about Family First and which often then provided more volunteers. For instance, Hilda Hanson, at her Mansfield Road salon volunteered to run five fashion shows to raise funds. The early Speakers' Group bore fruit for many years, including regular donors.

The role of volunteers and trainees sometimes blurs or reverses. A trainee may stay on as a volunteer or vice versa: sometimes trainees/volunteers have become staff. For example, when John Jarvis ran his own painting and decorating business, he volunteered to help with maintenance of properties. Eventually, he joined the staff, became Practical Services Manager and later Family First's Deputy Director and Director of Prospect Training Ltd (see below).

Family First's rooted ethos of inclusion has helped. Through its training and volunteering, people who felt excluded have found and developed confidence and sometimes become trainers themselves. Training opportunities develop and evolve in tune with many factors, including the needs/preferences of people who offer as volunteers, students or trainees; the current work needs within Family First; the culture (including prejudice) in wider society; the scale/type of local unemployment, and the breadth and accessibility of training opportunities on offer elsewhere locally.

Practical two-way learning

In 1973, I was asked to give evidence to the House of Commons Employment and Social Services Committee. This was because of the then very unusual and pro-active role Family First took in encouraging young mothers to think about training and what they might wish to achieve in their future. Margaret Bramall, Director of the National Council for the Unmarried Mother and her Child (later One Parent Families), told the Committee that women's training in Nottingham was ***"something exceptional, partly because of the very active work of Family First"*** .

Lone parents were among tenants/users of Family First for whom information and support towards training or completion of training were possible. For example in basic literacy; parenting skills; obtaining necessary examination grades for university entrance; nursing, or training to suit particular wishes e.g. car mechanic. Paid work for parents of young children has never been pushed but encouragement is offered to think towards an achieving future. Confidence building for often traumatised young people has happened in a myriad different ways.

For example, in 1997, after trauma due to violence, a mother and toddler moved into Mayholme/The Croft. The toddler attended Family First's day nursery. After a year, they moved into a permanent home. The mother obtained a place on a hairdressing course at Clarendon College in order to acquire a skill to make her independent. A requirement of the course was to buy necessary equipment which was impossible out of her state benefit: the sort of catch-22 situation that inhibits people moving forward. Family First's female support housing officer spent time finding a grant to cover the cost.

For 40 years, Family First has been highly regarded for its family orientated work.

Thirty years ago, The Croft Family Centre added a huge dimension to this work, offering training through informal and more formal methods. In 2005, The Croft Family Centre offered parenting classes; individual support, and opportunity to experience 'ordinary' family occasions.

"One of the things we try to do is to offer service users everyday normal opportunities, which are sometimes taken for granted . . . we do things out in the community with the parents and with the children in the nursery. For example, we once all went to Skegness on a coach and it was really nice. One of the tenants walking back to the coach said to me: Thanks a lot for that day, it has made me realise and appreciate how special my little boy is. I have had a lovely time with him and I'm going to do this sort of thing more often.'" Carmen Barnes (nee McPherson), Senior Service Manager, Children and Families (2003). She added: ***"I'm a hands on manager who will go out with staff on home visits, go into the nursery when needed . . . In this Service, we all know where we've come from: nobody's come from sitting in an office somewhere!"***

The day nursery has received support and helpful advice from both County Council and City Council day care supervisory staff, and from the Principal and staff at Waverley College, the nursery nurses' training college on Forest Road which later became part of Basford College, Nottingham. For example, Barbara Crosby when in charge of training nursery nurses at Basford College was a welcome professional adviser for the Family First day nursery. She always saw the potential in young mothers.

Social work students were placed with Family First soon after it opened, and later also at The Croft Family Centre. Nursery nurse NNEB students and other students were placed at The Family Centre day nursery from its inception in 1975. The Crescent Community Centre received social work trainees. Students sometimes came on placement from universities from outside as well as in Nottingham, and occasionally from overseas, including Helsinki, Finland. Students also came from organisations, e.g. the NSPCC.

Maria Dabrowksa, who later became Manager at Family First's Waterloo Crescent Community Centre, did her final student placement in 1975 with Family First. She said (2005) that the experience seriously turned her ideas around. She heard the then Personal Services Manager, Anna Block, tell a trainee statutory social worker to treat her client as a peer. ***"The social worker was aghast and said 'clients aren't peers',"*** says Maria. She thought about the issue, then did her diploma dissertation on the topic ***'Clients are Peers'***.

In its founding aims and objectives (1965), Family First stated its belief in the equality of each person, irrespective of background, faith or ethnicity. It practised this conviction in tenancy allocations and its outreach family work. Family First's early years coincided with significant growth in numbers of people from the Caribbean and the Indian sub-continent. Some sterling quiet work happened, often associated with distressed families who – soon after arrival – found themselves being compulsorily moved because of housing clearances. But they were ineligible for rehousing by the Council.

The pre-school second generation children were fairly represented in The Croft Family Centre day nursery, and staff applications/appointments from British ethnic minorities increased. In 1986, Family First issued a clear policy for combating racial harassment in housing and the Management Committee pledged its support to a scheme outlined by the Director, Angus Walker, which was to offer training opportunities for black people in housing management through housing associations. But after he left Family First, this policy failed for some years to affect housing staff appointments.

The Croft Family Centre initiated some excellent racial awareness training from the late 1980s, including ideas for use with children in the day nursery.

Dr Javid Khalique, who has been a senior trainer for both Nottinghamshire County Council and Nottingham City Council and was a member of Family First's Management Committee for some years, assisted Family First's work in developing its multi-cultural work in the late 1980s.

 Nottingham's Family First 1965-2005 ISBN 09550948 01

Speaking of that time, Dr Khalique said (2005): ***"The nursery nurses and nursery workers were a group of people who made a brilliant contribution . . . race awareness training didn't need to be confrontational . . . at The Croft Family Centre there was the most amazing group of people. They were (a) genuine and (b) curious, open to learning, concerned and cared for the children and the mums that they were in charge of."***

By 1993/94, having a member of staff who was a National Vocational Qualification [NVQ] Assessor enabled the assessment of Level 2/3 NVQ candidates at The Croft Family Centre, as well as placements of Diploma in Social Work students, NNEB students and Youth Training and Employment Training trainees. Nottinghamshire County Council's under 8s department congratulated (1995) The Croft Family Centre's staff team on the standards of child care at the day nursery. The same year, the Thomas Coram Research Unit's national study of quality in day care awarded The Croft Family Centre higher than national average results in all areas monitored. Special commendation was given for its multi-cultural work.

Family First tenants have sometimes become employees. For instance, the first (part-time) Furniture Service Manager was a former Mayholme/The Croft tenant.

Have reasons for volunteering changed?

In the chapter on Housing, I outline some work undertaken by volunteers in the early years. One group of volunteers (including tenants, students and neighbours) formed a lively fund-raising/social group which organised events, including many in the Community Room at The Croft. These events not only raised funds but also offered opportunity to meet both friends and newcomers. There were strenuous 'It's a Knockout' competitions held on the Elliott Durham School playing fields, sponsored walks, discos, the Annual Dance at the Sherwood Rooms or entertainment for a large crowd at the nightspot Alexandra's. Phil Moody was a key instigator of this group. Later she was on the staff as part-time Appeals Organiser and in the 1980s a manager with the Furniture and Clothing Service. Many people mourned her early death.

The vital role played by volunteers in the everyday life of Family First is highlighted in a letter from Joyce Jeffrey (2005). She recalled visiting young lone mothers in hospital after they gave birth. If a mother had no family/friends, she could decide if she wished a volunteer to look in at visiting times. Friendships often resulted. ***"S, whose baby was adopted by a relative, and another mum who had her baby used to come and visit us,"*** says Joyce Jeffrey. ***"S later married and sent me a card when her son was born and, in 1972, during a power cut she had to deliver her daughter herself."*** Joyce Jeffrey's husband, John, was an early member of Family First's Management Committee. He taught building construction at further education colleges and voluntarily advised Family First on property and construction issues.

Choosing to volunteer in a particular job is very personal. Sometimes people are volunteers because it is a way they can 'work' in the 'normal' world. I like the story of a member [former long-stay psychiatric hospital patient] of the Crescent Community Centre who, having learned skills and gained confidence as a volunteer, was able to take the opportunity of a short-term paid job at the Centre (see Neighbourhood Centres chapter).

This story also demonstrates the close relationship between work, training and volunteering. Trainees who work on placements for up to six months with Family First (often in its recycling services) are sometimes called volunteers. They are volunteers in that they are not paid by Family First (their financial support comes from another source).

'Real' volunteers offer to help because they have some time and energy to spare; want to try different sorts of work; wish to be needed; are curious and like new experiences; wish to do something helpful in society: there are many reasons why people get involved with Family First. The reasons for volunteering seem to be much the same as they were 30 and 40 years ago, but the circumstances are different.

There are fewer volunteers now than in earlier decades because more people, especially more women, are in paid work and because the environment within community organisations has changed as regulatory processes increasingly impinge upon them. The public sometimes perceives organisations like Family First as being funded and run by the statutory sector and not needing voluntary input. Although this is largely untrue, it is easy to see how that conclusion is made. There are many brilliant volunteers within Family First, but it is more difficult than in the earlier decades to create the momentum and involvement of significant numbers able to shoulder considerable responsibility. It is not so easy to have a volunteering ethos. Senior staff are incredibly busy doing their work and meeting the requirements of regulators[1]. Someone giving a talk about Family First to a women's group that considered offering support (2005) would have to mention the regulatory environment. This sadly can be a big turn-off!

I became Family First's President in 2004, a new voluntary role for me. I considered ways in which the good feeling that so many people have about Family First could be harnessed in an enjoyable way for furtherance of its work. It had to be a way in which people's ideas as well as their support could be valued. Family First's Board agreed that there was a positive role for a supporters' club. Then it became necessary for the Board to discuss Family First's future in terms of a possible strategic alliance with another housing association. So, it seemed unfair and inappropriate to ask people to commit time, ideas and effort to a supporters' club until there is more certainty about what that might entail.

"Family First trainees and volunteers are a vital resource for the organisation, and our training for them has benefited and now reflects Investors in People standards." Ann Cartwright, Chief Executive (2001).

1 Patrick Taylor, Director of Community Resources and Support Services, told me (2003): ***"We have a regulator from the Housing Corporation; we have an officer from the City Council; one from Supporting People; Ofsted regulators; mental health and Health Authority regulators: there are some ten different officers who regulate Family First"***

Management Committee/Board volunteers

Members of the Family First Management Committee/Board have always been volunteers even though, under current legislation, members could be paid. David Hunt, was recently followed as Chair by Janet Butler. He told me (2003): ***"If we are ever going to have an inclusive society then we need organisations like Family First which cross boundaries."***

Each Management Committee/Board member has contributed and does contribute in his or her own way and left a mark in ways that cannot always be seen until years later, as the following story will show. Margaret Clark joined Family First's Management Committee in 1967 for many years until moving from Nottingham. She died recently. Her son, the Revd Richard Clark, Vicar of St Andrews's Church, Nottingham, told me (2005) that his mother cared a great deal about the young women she met at Family First. A home economics lecturer, Margaret Clark helped Family First both in strategy and in hands-on practical ways. Richard Clark recalls that, with her and others, he was sometimes involved in helping to scrub out houses (the ones Family First rented from landlords: see Housing chapter).

He added: ***"From around the age of seven, my recollections of Family First are firstly of jumble sales and accompanying my parents to many musty halls. I was soon trusted to run the bric-a-brac stalls on these occasions and, afterwards, I would accompany my father to a rag-and-bone man behind Arkwright Street in the Meadows District. I remember the fun of ceilidh evenings in the Community Room at The Croft. These were led by volunteers Joy and Eric Foxley and enjoyed by tenants, volunteers and neighbours. I didn't quite understand what I was involved with at the time, but delighted that I was."***

Being a Management Committee/Board member increasingly became bound up with having views about, and needing to make decisions concerning, Housing Corporation imposed policy (see Appendix II). This interfered with the management process. In my view, Housing Corporation policies have often lacked consistency and wisdom. At some future time, the Corporation may well be called to account on a much broader canvas than Family First's. The errors that Family First made in housing policy under the watch of its third Director, Graham Wright, were in no small measure because the Management Committee did not know how to react to Housing Corporation pressures. These were inappropriate and, sadly, they were heeded! The current Board is working (voluntarily) to make good an untenable situation.

> Our Vision (2005)
>
> "family **first** is a charitable organisation delivering and developing integrated and innovative social housing and support services that empower local people in need to make choices."
>
> Members of the Board: Janet Butler, Chair; Geoff Culpin, Vice Chair; Richard Grosberg, Company Secretary; Janet Tennant; Mark Robinson; Stephen Hyde; Maria Iliffe; Craig Gilhooley; Cllr Mohammad Ibrahim, and Ann Cartwright (co-opted).

Community Service Volunteers

Before Family First could afford enough staff and whilst home-grown Nottingham volunteers were emerging, help came from Community Service Volunteers (CSV), the national organisation that places young people in useful organisations for several months. CSV is not to be confused with community service done by offenders as an alternative to a custodial sentence.

Margaret Kimbell, from Northampton, was Family First's first CSV. She lived with my family for three months at Mayholme in 1966 and was responsible for preparing accommodation for tenants and helping with general tasks at The Croft. Aged 18, she was a great help and found the experience valuable.

There was a succession of CSV trainees from the Metropolitan Police which sent them out of area for three-months into work where they met the public in different situations. These young men were the early 'mates' of Family First's furniture van driver. In some instances they were qualified to drive a van. One young man had to be returned to London: he had a penchant for sleeping in the van whenever unsupervised! The others were brilliant.

Volunteers on the 'wrong' side of the law

The young men from Lowdham Grange Borstal [now a prison] were involved with Family First early on. For example, their gymnastics team gave demonstrations at outdoor social events. Their next involvement was supervised work on property maintenance: window cleaning, painting and building skills usually learned in borstal. They were, almost invariably, hard working and thorough. Many experienced poor housing and family difficulties in childhood. They instinctively warmed to Family First's aims and ethos, and wanted to assist.

Prisoners in Nottingham Prison helped Family First through their woodworking activities, including toy making and small furniture projects.

The Trent Probation Hostel for young men opened on Woodborough Road not far from Mayholme/The Croft. Probationers sometimes attended social events at The Croft (in the large Community Room). They also became supervised property maintenance volunteers. One young man courted a Mayholme/The Croft tenant (also on probation). They married two years later and had their reception in the Community Room. Family First was family.

Community Service by offenders

The legal origin of community service orders lay in the Wootton Committee's report (1970) on non-custodial and semi-custodial treatment of offenders. Community service was one of several recommendations. On January 1st, 1973, as part of the provisions of the Criminal Justice Act 1972, a pilot experiment to try community service instead of a custodial sentence was started in six probation areas. One was Nottinghamshire. Family First was a lead organisation which received offenders and was successful in training and motivating them. Each offender usually did between 100-240 hours' community service. Many stayed in touch because they wanted to. Several trained as supervisors for the scheme. On arrival, they were usually 17-25 years of age. They tended to have committed property offences, offences against the person and motoring offences. Most were young men but a few were women. In a 12 month period 1973/1974, for example, 50 young men were placed with Family First.

The type of work available in Family First in the furniture workshop or doing house maintenance and rehabilitation was well-liked, and the offenders worked hard. It was no soft option which was sometimes a public criticism of the scheme.

The way Family First organised the training/work created unexpected successes. For example, one young man's pre-placement assessment before he came to Family First stated: ***"I don't think that he will complete Community Service and I think that it would be both to his advantage and to ours if he went back to the Courts and stated now that he was unlikely to be able to comply with the Order."*** AS.

John Harding, Senior Probation Officer in charge of the Nottinghamshire CSO scheme, wrote about the same young man afterwards: ***"He truly reversed expectations which were held of him . . . and as David admits he was hostile and indifferent and embittered about the whole idea of Community Service . . . The change seems to have taken place through two main factors – firstly, a placement with a voluntary organisation like Family First; secondly the inspiration and comradeship of people like Jack Pooler and John Jarvis, the supervisors at Family First. . . He became absorbed in the work and the aims of Family First, in its endeavours to meet the needs of those who are homeless, particularly amongst single parent families. In his growing curiosity about the organisation he began to ask questions and to seek further involvement for himself[2]."***

What made Family First placements successful was a complete lack of 'them and us' and, at the same time, ensuring that the quality of the work and training made people feel they had achieved something. One former offender said: ***"He [John Jarvis, Family First] is a man who accepted lads on Community Service and gave them a variety of work, some interesting, some not so interesting, all hard. He too has a confidence about him, a confidence that only comes from believing in what he is doing[3]."***

Having examined the progress of community service in its experimental areas, the Home Office Research Unit decided community service orders were viable and, in consequence, probation and after-care committees throughout England and Wales were asked to provide community service schemes as soon as possible after August 1st, 1975 for suitable offenders.

Family First continued to be involved with offenders on community service placements until the 1990s.

Training in schools

For some years, Family First undertook training projects on housing in two comprehensive schools: Elliott Durham (the neighbourhood school for Mayholme/The Croft) and the Frank Wheldon in Carlton. I wrote a training pack. One of us went into school once a week for six weeks to introduce senior pupils to a range of housing options available when in future they set up home. The idea of thinking ahead was often a new concept to them: for instance, putting their name on a Council housing list at age 18, pending a time when they needed a home.

As part of the training, pupils viewed plans of a property being rehabilitated by Family First and visited it to see work in progress. They learned about planning regulations, home improvement grants, kitchen planning, cupboard space, redecorating, and budgeting for furniture, etc. They measured up for curtains, helped to select fabrics and sometimes made the

[2] In *Community Service by Offenders (The Nottingham Experiment)* edited by John Harding [National Association for the Care and Resettlement of Offenders. 1974], p. 19

[3] Ibid, p. 49

curtains as a project in school. Pupils were sometimes involved in decorating and gardening. A few later did voluntary work for Family First.

As Family First's workload increased it was not possible, on a regular basis, to sustain this particular training which was regarded as valuable by schools. They did not feel able to continue it themselves. However, links were continued and developed with schools whenever possible. The Player Comprehensive School, for example, in 1977 helped to make notice-boards and delivery boxes for the Crescent Community Centre and properties in the Waterloo Crescent rehabilitation scheme. Later, due to the changing pressures on schools, the extent of their community involvement lessened.

Schools and sixth form colleges, as well as university students, have sometimes adopted Family First as 'their' special fund-raising project. For instance, in 1996 students at Bilborough Sixth Form College chose Family First hostels as their charity and raised the amazing sum of £5,239 for Family First through various events including a 178-mile Offa's Dyke walk on the borders of England and Wales.

Practical Services

Practical Services was the overall name used for many years for all aspects of housing maintenance; work done in-house on property conversions/rehabilitation; the Furniture and Clothing Service, and training of volunteers and trainees.

In 1977, there were two staff and eight trainees doing property work. Then major increase of unemployment nationally led Practical Services to organise employment training initiatives. Funding was obtained from the Manpower Services Commission. The first initiative was a youth training project, the Nottingham Inter-Community Enterprise (NICE), based on Huntingdon Street. There were up to 200 trainees and 35 staff. It provided a training base for the building trades, workshop activities, work placements and practical projects.

By 1981, there was adult training in the Family First Projects Agency, based at Radford Mill and Kilbourn Street, undertaking the same balance of activities with 600 trainees and 75 staff. The Beaver Workshop (1982) was a Probation Service-linked project on Raleigh Street. This involved two staff and 12 adult trainees, manufacturing and installing ramps and rails, etc to assist people with disabilities.

There was a significant growth in scale of the training work from 1984 to 1988 involving both youth and adult training. Two sizeable projects were linked to Stanton Ironworks, Ilkeston, to assist with new jobs and retraining for both younger people and older ones losing their jobs. One project was in Chesterfield (work placements and building projects) and one in Derby city centre (adult literacy, life and social skills and work placements). In 1988, enterprise training for new businesses was launched initially at Radford Mill.

At the busiest time, these training and employment related projects employed 200 staff and 1,000 trainees. Today's high employment is very different from the near-past time of devastating unemployment due not least to closure of traditional industries. In and around Nottingham these included Stanton Ironworks, coal mines, much of the textile industry and Raleigh.

Family First benefited from work undertaken by supervised trainees on these projects. For example, they built an extension and rehabilitated the warehouse building at 375, Alfred Street North; did the conversion work to the Crescent Community Centre on Waterloo Road; alterations to Miscellany in Mapperley to assist the pop-in project, and numerous housing repairs.

Family First Training Services Ltd

From 1986 to 1988, a lot changed in Family First. It is important to understand why, not least because lessons can always be learned that might help to inform the future in some way. The reasons for this change were complex and included at least three factors:-

Firstly, as early as 1981, Angus Walker, Family First's Director, wrote a paper and tried to open up a pro-active debate about the role of members of the Management Committee. He suggested that in an organisation like Family First, members should have more than a theoretical understanding about Family First. ***"I can see and understand the need for detachment,"*** he said, ***"but not at the expense of knowledge and awareness."*** He suggested issues needing attention. At the time, most of the members were relatively new and the Housing sub-group of the Management Committee became increasingly dominant because of an assumption that it was the 'main' committee. It included a significant proportion of members whose focus was dominated by what I call the 'overt' business model.

By the late 1980s, Government rhetoric and policy were favouring the 'overt' business model which became a national culture. The 'overt' business model was confidently proclaimed as the path to efficiency, it infiltrated all aspects of public and community life, but it too often produced 'business people' with little practical business acumen. Even if they had failed in running businesses, 'business people' were found running all sorts of bodies! In the Family First context, the 'overt' business model led to a failure to understand how complex people organisations like Family First run successfully, especially when many of the people involved come from often excluded groups!

Secondly, when the Housing Corporation started to question the status and scale of Family First's in-house training enterprise, the Management Committee rejected the Director's preference for it to become part of a group structure[4]. This type of structure, which favoured the social enterprise model, was increasingly used by registered social landlords running non-housing operations. Instead, in 1986, Family First Training Services Ltd was set up as a separate organisation but with a common Management Committee and some staff in common for a further two years.

Thirdly, the Housing Corporation by 1988 was exerting pressure for Family First Training Services Ltd to be totally detached, despite having separate accounts and no financial conflict of interest with the Housing Corporation's stake in Family First's housing. The Management Committee was told that the Housing Corporation, under its policy document on group structures, regarded Family First Training Services Ltd as an unsatisfactory structure. The Management Committee was persuaded that complete separation was best. One member of the Management Committee at the time told me (2005) that two weeks after the complete separation, the Housing Corporation told him it had actually been unnecessary.

So, in 1988, there was a complete separation of Family First Training Services Ltd from Family First. The new name of the training company was Prospect Training Ltd, with John Jarvis (formerly Family First's Deputy Director) as Director. It moved to 3, Broadway in the Lace Market, Nottingham, a building of 20,000 sq ft which staff and trainees converted into a multi-purpose suite of offices, training rooms, conference centre and catering centre using its own resources and a grant from Nottingham City Council.

With hindsight, had Family First Training Services Ltd been part of a group structure, as a social enterprise it could – almost certainly – have flexibly adjusted to changes with mutual benefit both to itself and to Family First over future years. Trainees from Prospect Training Ltd did sometimes undertake work within Family First and there were working links between the two organisations.

The complexities of 1986-1988, initiated by Housing Corporation changes in policy, created considerable differences of opinion in Family First's Management Committee between those who saw Angus Walker as ***'an unusually creative Director'*** and those who felt he should be swayed by the 'overt' business way of thinking. Things came to a head when

4 A Group Structure enabled certain non-housing activities to be separated from the housing function and, therefore, not regulated by the Housing Corporation

a Management Committee member with 'overt' business thoughts acted with fervent speed when signing cheques. Without asking the Director to explain the (explainable) situation of an apparently looming £50,000 overdraft, this member phoned other members of the Committee: they did not all accept the implications. One rightly said that ***"all members were equally responsible"*** for a situation which was due to the inadequacies of a previous accountant and which had been pointed out to them. Family First was, in fact, securely funded up to 1990.

Angus Walker left in May 1988. As described in Appendix II, he regrets that Family First Training Services Ltd became detached. Staff were disheartened at the way events were handled and, when changes to staff were introduced by the new Director in the early 1990s, there were considerable staff and, interestingly, tenant protests.

So, in 1988, Prospect Training Ltd set out on its own. It continued to do valuable work but, within two years, the Training and Enterprise Councils [TECs] were taking the place of the Manpower Services Commission. John Jarvis told me (2005): ***"At this point there was an important shift from the common understanding that a significant number of trainees either had some form of special need or training need. Contracts became increasingly 'outcome' based and, at the same time, arrears funding was introduced [the 'overt' business model!] leaving many organisations in funding difficulties . . . The Management Committee and I grew concerned that the new climate reduced our capacity to offer genuine opportunities to the most vulnerable."***

Prospect Training Ltd went into company administration in 1992 and, whilst achieving useful work to the end, closed in 1994. John Jarvis added (2005): ***"We had started with an emphasis on community development, working with the most vulnerable and supporting the voluntary sector. Commercial pressures and less than philanthropic attitudes were such that these principles were increasingly difficult to sustain."***

There is no doubt that during the years of high unemployment, the initiatives mentioned above played a front-line role in delivering skills and, importantly, hope and confidence to young people facing an uncertain employment future and to older people displaced from their jobs.

> Some energetic volunteers were created by the Great Bike Ride of 23 miles organised by Nottinghamshire County Council Leisure Services and the benefiting charities. Each year benefited four charities and each charity chosen benefited for several years. Family First benefited for four years ending in 1997 when over £8,000 was raised for Family First.

Development of training, trainees and volunteers in recent years

In addition to trainees and volunteers working directly for Family First, it has received placements from local training agencies for work-based training for over 25 years. There have always been some Family First staff who initially started as trainees. In 2001/02, for example, three trainees gained staff positions in Family First through an open recruitment process.

Terry Campbell, now Service Manager of Community Resources, joined as a trainee and was employed from 1990. He told me (2004) there were opportunities for more trainees in addition to the six currently working with the Furniture Service. They worked four days a week and spent one day a week with their training agency, for example, Better Employment Skills Training Company [BESTCO]. Each trainee usually spends up to six months with Family First.

Mike Toner also came as a trainee, was employed in 1995, became Warehouse Supervisor, then Placement Manager (placing trainees throughout Family First) and Health and Safety Co-ordinator. He qualified as an internal assessor so that trainees could take NVQ qualifications. He creates training programmes for individuals on placement and new volunteers throughout the organisation, including The Croft Family Centre, the Amity centre and central administration. Volunteers are asked what skills they have and what type of work they wish to undertake. They have an induction that includes all aspects of Family First's work.

In 2000, there were 23 core volunteers working in the Community Resources Division (Furniture Service, Kidstuff and shops). There were 78 training placements during the year and more than 40 of those trainees achieved NVQ Level 1 & 2 in warehousing, retailing, administration or information technology.

Repairing electric equipment added to training opportunities in 2002. The Community Resources Division provided 76 training places for people aged over 16. Of these, 20% gained full-time employment afterwards.

Unemployed people are often the long-term unemployed, said Mike Toner (2005). ***"We have people in their forties who have never worked a day in their life, but when you see them work they are like 'diamonds'. Our biggest job has always been – in the warehouse certainly – in building confidence first. Their educational standard can be poor, about three-quarters couldn't read or write. We get people in and you can barely get their name from them, but you go through the training process and, more often than not, these people turn out to be the real grafters. ... Some of them really blossom in this atmosphere. We tend to start with humour: humour breaks down so many barriers. It's amazing when they realise work is not all serious! . . . They all come back to see us, even those who are still unemployed come back to see us."***

Training in Family First is ongoing. Mike Toner told me, for example: ***"Every member of staff who works here will be first aid qualified by 2006."***

Comment

Family First has a 40-year tradition of proving that people best suited to responsible jobs are not necessarily only those directly trained for those jobs. They can be people determined to become the best possible by constantly learning and developing skills to do their job well and, importantly, to understand the context in which it is done. Exactly the same principle applies to volunteers, trainees and all connected to Family First.

To be open to learning can take courage, as it did for a young institutionalised single mother when she and her baby were living at Mayholme/The Croft. She started to attend literacy classes because she wanted to help her baby son with homework when he reached secondary school. To have a mother able neither to read nor write was not something she intended for him.

Playschemes in school holidays

School holiday playschemes for the five to 13-year-olds were organised by Family First from the mid 1970s, first on the Elliott Durham Comprehensive School premises and later at the Walter Halls School. When Family First set up its annual Easter and summer school holiday playschemes, they were especially welcomed by parents who were working and/or those who welcomed the stimulating opportunities the playschemes offered their children. The emphasis was on hobbies and sports, plus outings. Over the years the duration of playschemes and the children's ages varied. In 1991, the summer playscheme was for two weeks for 60 children aged five to 11. In 1992, it was for four weeks. In 1994, it was for two-and-a-half weeks for 50 children. The length of time and number of children able to attend depended on the funding that could be found. Skilled staff had to be found and paid. Somehow, Family First playschemes always happened until around the mid-1990s when it became more difficult to find the funding. Funding sources have become more 'outcome' orientated. Offering children and young people experience and opportunities is hard to quantify in terms of results. It takes imagination and skill to determine whether something like a playscheme is value for money. But children remember for life what they enjoyed doing at a summer playscheme.

Nottingham's Family First 1965-2005 ISBN 09550948 01

SUMMARY

This 40-year history of Family First raises at least one important question. What is the role of innovative local community based self-help organisations in the early 21st Century?

From 1965, Family First broke the stereotypical mould of viewing as problems young lone mothers; young people on probation; the single homeless of all ages, and all sorts of families who ran into a crisis period in their lives. Family First was prepared to find innovative ways to work alongside people. In early statements, it often referred to the need to prevent an individual's or a family's crisis becoming a long-term problem.

Family First also explored practical social and voluntary/paid employment avenues for people leaving long-term psychiatric hospitals and joining 'the community', and those who were long-term unemployed. Family First viewed many people in these groups as having been involuntarily institutionalised. Indeed, it was running an imaginative drop-in centre for patients of Mapperley (Psychiatric) Hospital and volunteers years before Care in the Community was policy.

Family First soon achieved outstanding work, offering a holistic range of flexible opportunities with new forms of housing, neighbourhood centres, child care within a family centre (a new idea then), support networks, training, provision of practical back-up (e.g. furniture and clothing services) and much more. Some people's testimonies are included in the book: there are many, many more which space disallows.

Today's Family First staff, some 55 in number, work with the conviction that treating people with respect is a must. That respect includes a belief in the ability of those families and individuals they work with to create their own positive future. Staff skill and determination are impressive in view of their experience of the relentless increase in inappropriate regulation, imposed policies (stemming from Government) and the stop-start short-term funding that so often creates uncertainties. This book has described some of these problems, which – alas – are endemic and not peculiar to Family First. There is a huge social and economic cost to the nation resulting from short-term thinking, imposed ever-changing policies and procedures, and over-regulation.

The Housing Corporation will not allow any steady development in Family First's housing work because as a small specialist housing provider it is not a preferred partner. But the Corporation carries on regulating it, including the imposition of what is now called the 'efficiency agenda'.

Government rhetoric is in favour of neighbourhoods, despite much evidence to the contrary. Family First's work – as we have seen – created a practical and successful neighbourhood focus for many families and individuals who either belonged to stereotyped 'outsider' groups or who were experiencing extreme difficulties. But in recent years, such a concept of inclusive neighbourhoods has been and is being undermined because of the 'best value' regime which can designate and quantify help for people only as if they were isolated units: like tins on a supermarket shelf.

The imposed killing-off of a brilliant partnership between Family First and the City Council's Housing Department led to families in crisis losing the opportunity for prompt housing help with Family First for as long as needed (usually around two years) with the associated benefits of support, optional social activities and more. By the time they moved on into Local Authority housing or that of a large housing association, they had determined how to progress in their lives, had networks of friends and, if desired, a continuing link with Family First.

The Croft Family Centre, from being a neighbourhood centre which included services and support for families in crisis, became in later years a centre working entirely for families and children 'in need'. June Allen, Nottinghamshire County Council's Senior Professional Officer for under-fives and member of a strong professional group which supported Family First's day nursery, believed passionately in the value of the preventative capability of the day nursery. She stressed (1987) it should not become a crisis centre. She and her colleagues recognised the value for the children and their parents of mixing with a cross-section of all families. Now we have a society in which funding policies deliberately divide people into those 'in need' and those who are not. Where is the recognition that people may both need help and be able also to offer it?

Parents and children undoubtedly benefit from their connection with Family First and the quality of its family work is widely recognised as very high indeed. Family Centre staff maintain a holistic approach and, if they were not there, I do not know what would happen to some of the children who now spend time at the day nursery. Nevertheless, they and their families deserve to be mixing in a wider social setting, as June Allen recognised a long time ago. That mix in a normal situation like a day nursery within a family centre leads to genuine inclusion.

'Care in the Community' was a huge leap forward for thousands of people who had spent a long time in psychiatric hospitals. They included many who were hospitalised because – in the 1940s, 1950s and even 1960s – they had learning difficulties. We saw earlier in the book how people with this background, and many others who lived in the neighbourhood, enjoyed Family First's Crescent Community Centre on Waterloo Road. It had to close largely because it lost modest funding which helped to provide the space and skills which created a warm and stimulating atmosphere. Mental Health funding was eventually withdrawn, for use only for a 'dedicated' service. So what about Care in the Community?

Now Family First's dedicated Amity project is in a separate building owned by an NHS primary care trust that needs funds. Valuable work is achieved because staff maintain the Family First ethos, but they fear for the project's future and especially for members who may need two or three years before they learn to trust staff. They surely deserve continuity? Will the property be sold to release its value? Where would members, who live in registered homes, go each day?

As we have seen, imposed policies and regulations are increasingly creating the very social isolation (leading often to social exclusion) which – in theory – they usually purport to be helping to solve. The following example illustrates this confused and impractical thinking. It is necessary to remember that Family First never set out to provide only housing. The Housing Corporation seems sometimes to be obsessed with the desire to regulate that part of Family First's work which is not housing (and in which it has no financial stake). In 2000 Ita Cooke, then a Regulation Manager in the Housing Corporation's Leicester office, was trying to define whether Family First's Furniture Service and its white goods recycling scheme would qualify as 'social housing' within the Housing Corporation regulatory framework.

"Our interpretation," she wrote to Ann Cartwright, Chief Executive, ***"is that such activities would qualify as 'social housing' if they are specifically linked to a defined regeneration area – which will usually be defined for funding purposes such as Single Regeneration Budget (SRG) or New Deal for Communities. I am not clear from your letter that this is the case."*** In other words, was the Furniture Service and white goods scheme limited to certain postcodes or New Deal districts? I cite this as yet another example where regulation (following Government policy) attempts to narrow the focus and divide people: in this case perhaps suggesting these Family First services might be limited to 'deprived' areas. What a nonsense this all is. Why is the Housing Corporation even thinking about this issue when it has no stake in the Furniture Service and its accounts are separate?

Interestingly, its recycling services are a key area of the work of Family First's which – for 40 years – has not suffered imposed regulation of its management methods by any outside agency, although the Housing

Corporation has tried to set a limit on its growth. It has run (in spite of other restraints, e.g. too limited warehouse space) a service recognised as of great value to Nottingham and its surrounding areas. It is significant that, when the Family First Board is in discussions about a possible strategic alliance with Leicester Housing Assocation-ASRA, Family First's main attractions include its recycling services and its skills in a wide range of family and community care.

So what of the future?

Patrick Taylor, Director of Family First Community Resources and Support Services and also Deputy Chief Executive, hoped (2005) ***"Family First will be in a position to maintain its range of projects that currently provide invaluable services to many thousands of people in Nottingham and Nottinghamshire . . . There is without doubt potential to develop all of the non-housing projects".*** He sees the need for development of social enterprises.

Ann Cartwright, Chief Executive, talking about Family First's future, said (2005): ***"The concept of local solutions for and involving local people seems to be getting lost in the drive to build more houses. However, unless you are one of the Housing Corporation's preferred partners you cannot even play that game. At the same time the regulatory regime gets stronger, putting more and more requirement and restriction on what a registered social landlord can do.***

"The level and volume of regulation are the same regardless of size – a 'one size fits all' approach. Small local community based registered social landlords like Family First are being squeezed out.

". . . The only way we can protect ourselves against the 'drive for efficiency' is to find a way of getting bigger. So we need to find an alternative option and that is likely to involve joining forces with another like-minded organisation. The trick here will be to join with someone who is large enough to be a player and small enough to believe in local accountability and who shares our values and ethos. It's a tall order . . ."

What is the legacy of Family First's 40 years to date?

The fact that Family First still dynamically exists is a tribute to all involved. It has survived because of its robust non-patronising concern for people of whatever background, beliefs and needs. In spite of all sorts of vicissitudes, Family First has steadfastly ignored stereotypical views about people with whom it works. That legacy is also carried forward in many lives and workplaces. It has influenced thinking in the UK and overseas.

Family First's major legacy, however, is not an organisation but its people. Over the past 40 years, it has worked with many thousands of tenants and other people who have used its many services. Staff; volunteers; trainees; students; neighbours; all who have supported Family First by fund-raising, donations and legacies: and those who have given furniture and clothing have all played an important part in the Family First story. I have been fortunate to work alongside some of these people. In the years 1978-2005, I have met and heard from many more who have been associated with Family First. The following remarks of one of them summarise Family First's legacy: ***"It was a special time when I worked there [in the Croft Family Centre]. I learned different ways of looking at things and doing things. I keep that possibility with me whatever I do."***

On December 8th, 2005, the Board announced that Family First was in discussion with the LHA-ASRA housing and regeneration group as a way forward. The Press Release stated: ***"The planned strategic alliance between LHA-ASRA and Family First will deliver services to over 11,000 homes in the East Midlands, London and the Home Counties. Group members expect to benefit from the associated enhancement opportunities in community care, further investment and procurement."***

At a meeting of Family First staff on December 9th, 2005, it was stressed that the organisation was at the beginning of the process of talks, not the end. Staff were positive, but stressed concerns that services currently offered by Family First should continue for local people in Nottingham and its surrounding areas.

APPENDIX I

Proposed Use of The Croft Family Centre

Extracts from a paper by Ruth I Johns, Director. June 1972

The Family Centre will provide an extension of the existing community work based at The Croft which, as well as being its administrative HQ and providing accommodation for eight tenants, has a community lounge[1] and kitchen used by tenants, volunteers (including many young people) and neighbours. This use is mainly informal – people meet and chat; but organised meetings are sometimes arranged either by Family First or its tenants (e.g. tenants formed a Red Cross Group in 1971 which met weekly in the Community Room). There is a Resident Family at The Croft to co-ordinate all activities. Occasional social events are run by young people e.g. poetry and folk evenings and are enjoyed by a very mixed audience including neighbours. Neighbourhood participation has always been encouraged and, before the new project gets under way, we will be asking local residents if they would like to form a group with some management interest in the project.

The site is conveniently placed within a quarter of a mile of the St Ann's Redevelopment Area, adjoining the Caunton Avenue development and in an area of very mixed housing including multi-occupied and owner-occupied. Main bus routes run close to hand at frequent intervals. It is only one mile from the City Centre.

Day Nursery

. . . The provision of a Day Nursery at present is a vital missing link in meeting needs for many families known to us. The Day Nursery will be able to cope with the needs of less stable tenants and clients or those referred to us – often we would like a child placed in satisfactory day care to enable the mother to discover and learn what is involved in child care. We would envisage reserving a proportion of places for children whose parents needed help in understanding the needs of their children. We find a small but significant proportion of young deserted wives, for example, who show temporary rejection of their children after the desertion of the father and the children need some protection without complete separation from their mother who can be helped to come to terms with her own initial feelings of hostility and rejection without emotionally harming her children. Some single mothers also need to understand the needs of their children. Girls reared institutionally may say they want to keep their child, keep their child, and really love their child yet have no understanding of how to deal with his/her development. Guidance, which is not labelled but built in to a pattern of community caring and help, is far more acceptable and effective than direct 'teaching'.

The Day Nursery will be run with family groups and with a trained staff. It has been designed after consultation with Mrs June Allen, Supervisor of Nottingham City's Day Nurseries, and visits to Matrons of several day nurseries run by Local Authorities and Voluntary Agencies both locally and further afield as well as on the basis of the most up-to-date knowledge of the needs of deprived families with small children . . .

. . . Tenants who are using the nearest City Day Nursery have at least a half-a-mile walk to and from Nursery on steep hills. Many do not take up work or training because of the practical difficulties involved in a long walk, followed often by several changes of bus to get to their destination. The number of priority places at the proposed Nursery will be approximately three-quarters but the reasons for being 'priority' will be mixed i.e. not all from families where parental care is questionable, not all of motherless or fatherless families. But three-quarters will be there because of urgent need or because a child at nursery enables a parent to train or work and become more competent as a person and parent. The remainder of the children will come from neighbourhood families.

[1] And a general purpose room that became known as the community room after the original Community Room was divided into office space in 1994

Young people

The Family Centre is urgently needed as an extension of our present work. Much of our work is preventative and increasingly it involves young people in community help, when otherwise they would have nothing else useful to do with their time. Such young people may be unemployed, disabled, out-patients of mental hospitals or on probation. We also have the help of school children doing projects and doing voluntary work out of school hours, and a lot of help from students. Increasingly children (8 – 15-year-olds) from the Caunton Avenue Local Authority development which borders The Croft are asking us to involve them in our activities. The success of involving young people in community work is not only that they do a useful job but that they often find a worthwhile reason for living through doing it . . . Most of the activity concerning young people will not be done at the Centre but out and about (often at properties Family First is converting) – the Centre will provide the base and 'focus'. . .

Parents

As mentioned in the section on Day Nurseries, many parents find their way to The Croft and use it as a meeting place. Some get involved in the management of Family First or organising of social events: some use it as a base from which to offer voluntary and/or neighbourhood help (e.g. shopping for the local elderly or infirm), some as a place 'to walk to and have a rest'. Whatever the reason for coming, there is no doubt that it serves a useful purpose. At present there is insufficient room and more space is needed. Once the Day Nursery is built, there would be room, for example, for a small playgroup in the existing building if a group of parents wanted a place to visit so their children could play together for regular sessions each week.

Elderly

Elderly people in the area – and there are many living alone or with relatives as well as others living in Local Authority or voluntarily-run Homes or flatlet schemes – have been involved in Family First work. For example, tenants regularly visit two Homes each Christmas to carol-sing, others have shopped or done errands in times of illness, and some elderly neighbours are themselves volunteers for Family First. When one old lady died recently, local tenants of Family First sent flowers to: ***The good old-fashioned Granny who we liked."*** Family First volunteers helped to provide fuel for old people from trees felled from Family First properties during last winter's electricity crisis. The building of a Family Centre would free space in the existing building for the elderly to visit and have a meal once/twice a week. Meals could be sent out to others in the area if this was – after consultation with other City agencies – thought to be helpful. Some of the elderly are of the 'old school' and having lived in the area from the time it was 'very select' seem to warm more to the help and support offered via community self-help than they would at the least hint of ***'being done good to'.***

APPENDIX II

A brief summary of the Housing Corporation's impact on Family First's housing and non-housing work

NB 'Development' in Housing Corporation language means increase of housing units

Housing

It is important to understand the changing role of the Housing Corporation over the past three decades. Its policies – as determined by successive governments – have affected Family First's ability to achieve the potential of its aims and objectives.

There is space to offer readers only an awareness of the nature of the 'partnership' of Family First and the Housing Corporation following the Housing Act 1974 which led to the Corporation's powerful involvement with housing associations.

The Housing Corporation, a Quango [quasi-autonomous non-government organisation], was set up a decade earlier in 1964. Initially, the Housing Corporation's function was limited. It existed to promote and assist housing societies (registered under the Industrial and Provident Societies Act 1965) to provide cost rent and co-ownership housing. Cost rent and co-ownership proved successful in bridging the gap between market rented accommodation and owner-occupation, but development of this form of tenure declined after 1972 due to increased land and building costs.

The Housing Finance Act 1972 set out three new forms of subsidy for housing associations and the Housing Act 1974 marked a fundamental change in the history of the voluntary housing association movement.

The 1974 Act was deemed necessary because, especially for the growing number of large housing associations, existing financial support was insufficient to deal with increased management and maintenance costs, and the statutory limitations of rents. Along with the higher level of financial support, the Housing Corporation was charged with the dual tasks of controlling the housing association movement through a new system of registration and ***"of encouraging the development of registered housing associations so that they could play their full part in implementing the Government's housing policies[1]".***

Interestingly and significantly, at the time the Housing Corporation registered Family First (1975), its housing finances, 10 years after it started, balanced. Until 1971/72, when modest Exchequer subsidy [via the Department of the Environment] became available, Family First received no statutory capital assistance in purchasing, rehabilitating or converting properties.

When it registered with the Housing Corporation in 1975, Family First's model was commended. The model was to use housing as only one tool in a portfolio of services for families and individuals in housing/social difficulty. I was regularly asked by the Housing Corporation if other organisations could visit Family First to see its work.

However, over time, the Housing Corporation evolved (through successive Government legislation) into a regulatory body and thus, unusually, was entrusted with the dual role of both investor and regulator. For example, details of the Corporation's monitoring role covered in Circular 20/18 (October 1981) changed its role from management consultancy to supervisory. By the mid-1980s, it was clearly being stated that the future of the housing association movement ***"may well depend upon the ability and willingness of associations to adapt to changes in emphasis and direction seen by the Government as part of its overall housing policies[2]".***

The Housing Act 1974 also imposed an extended role upon local authorities as

[1] Manual of Housing Association Finance [The Chartered Institute of Public Finance & Accountancy. 1985]

[2] Ibid

agents of central government to make increased funding allocations to local housing associations. As a result, local authorities increasingly viewed the role of the small specialist housing associations (as well as the large ones) as that of providing housing for Local Authority housing list referrals. These changes took no account of existing good mutual working arrangements: however, those between Nottingham City Housing Department and Family First (see Housing chapter) held for many more years.

In 1987, Angus Walker, then Family First Director, reported to Family First's Management Committee on his meeting with the Housing Corporation. There were three main points:-

- From May 5th, 1989, housing associations would be required to use private finance to fund their development programmes.
- Assured tenancies would apply to new developments and re-lets and would substantially increase rents, ***"putting the majority of our tenants into considerable trouble".***
- Local Authority tenants would be given the right to choose their landlord and housing associations would be expected to play the key role in responding to this initiative.

Once again the Housing Corporation's role was fundamentally changed and housing associations were simply expected to dance to the new tune. It was the enforced move to all assured tenancies which destroyed Family First's close practical working relationship with Nottingham City Housing Department (described in the Housing chapter).

As the Housing Corporation's regulatory function grew, undoubtedly for some years it unduly influenced the housing strategy of the Family First Management Committee and Family First's third Director, Graham Wright, who joined just before the Housing Act in 1988. This, as we saw above, was the time when the Housing Corporation required housing associations to use private finance to develop their housing programmes. The Housing Corporation wrote (1989): ***"The Corporation is facing a serious risk of reaching its cash limit very early in the calendar year 1990. If this happens, we shall be unable under any circumstances to advance Housing Association Grant [HAG] or loans to associations."***

So the Housing Corporation, which was not very good at minding its own affairs, was given enhanced power of regulation over housing associations!

With hindsight, it might have been better if Family First, as its senior housing staff at the time believed, had ridden out the storm without attempting to go for anything other than suitable growth in terms of its agreed aims and objectives. It is always difficult to strike a balance between standing up to authority and compromising with it. At that time, Family First tried to keep in favour with the prevailing ideas of top-down policies whilst simultaneously its social housing policy was frustrated by them.

For example In 1992, Graham Wright wrote to the Chief Executive of the Housing Corporation: ***"As predicted by housing association 'experts', the introduction of private finance and limited Housing Association Grant input has increased rents and reduced space and building quality standards . . . When will we be allowed to just get on with what we are best at – providing and managing social housing? Constant changes in policy and procedures continually disrupt the very valuable resources of housing associations and a proven ability to produce the goods."***

But the desire to please authority prevailed (i.e. to be seen as 'business' orientated). For example, the Family First Housing Sub-Committee recommendation in 1991 stated that all referrals for permanent housing with Family First should be via the City Council's nomination procedures. A Family First Management Committee minute read: ***"Family First will be able to contribute to the Council's initiatives to reduce homelessness in a very positive way. In the light of Sir George Young's[3] recent statement urging Housing Associations to increase the proportion of lettings which go to nominees defined by Local Authorities as homeless, this is obviously an important factor."***

[3] Sir George Young was Minister for Housing and Planning

It would be unfair to blame the Housing Corporation for all the difficulties encountered by Family First to develop its housing work in accordance with its aims and objectives. But any organisation is less innovative, less managerially effective, and more expensive to run once time and energy are spent not on managing and executing its practical work but on conforming to over-regulation.

Brian Kingdom, Housing Manager at Family First (1978-1991), told me (2005): ***"Richard Best [now Lord Best] of the National Federation of Housing Associations said it was time for small specialist housing associations to batten down the hatches. They could not compete with the large associations, but should manage their stock well and do what they were good at for people. The housing and personal services management team at Family First felt we could have survived that way.***

"Family First was in a strong position because of the housing stock of the early years secured outright with [non-statutory] grant funds and donations. But the new Director and the Management Committee – under pressure from the Housing Corporation – went for development [of housing]. As soon as more private finance was available, Family First took on mortgages it could not sustain."

He added: ***"I followed Cliff Lewis as Housing Manager. He wasn't from a housing background but I learned so much from him in the way he dealt with people. He understood them, never patronised and dealt brilliantly with sometimes potentially quite difficult situations. It's the interaction with people that is the most important thing and I've never forgotten that perspective."*** Brian Kingdom is now Deputy Director and Resource Service Manager of the Nottingham Hostels Liaison Group.

In its 1993 Annual Report, Family First stated that it had an allocation from the Housing Corporation to purchase 10 existing 'satisfactory' houses from April 1993, and made a submission for approval to the Corporation on May 13th. This is only one of many indications of accepting whatever the Housing Corporation offered without incisive questioning of the value of the offer.

The Chairperson said in her report (1995): ***"We have continued to develop the housing stock, although it becomes more competitive each year with the Housing Corporation cutting back on public funding, expecting us to find money from elsewhere and provide housing with less capital. This means a lowering of standards and higher rents. We want to provide low cost housing for those in the greatest need and at rents our tenants can afford, but the goal posts get moved so often it is quite a task.***

"At present, we are having to look at 'existing satisfactories' rather than new build, i.e. houses that do not need a great deal spending on them. For the first time, we are doing a short-life scheme."

The 'existing satisfactories' created much of the pepper-potting referred to in the Housing chapter. These properties may have been habitable (i.e. 'satisfactory') from day one, but they brought with them disproportionate future maintenance and upgrading costs. And the Corporation's view on standards soon changed dramatically.

For example, on the subject of Family First's quality of housing the Housing Corporation (2000) reported: ***"There were no adverse findings. The quality of housing is generally of a good standard with all the essential standards as well as some of the recommended standards."***

Then the Corporation's Decent Homes Standards initiative became a new enforced guideline. It changed the Corporation's perceptions of the quality of housing stock, which it had found satisfactory to that point. For an association that has a well-developed maintenance programme for its housing stock, these arbitrarily imposed decisions, with implied threats for non-compliance, do little to help to create a sustained climate of co-operation between 'partners'. Family First's 2002 Housing Corporation inspection report stated: ***"Some 78% of the association's stock is over 20 years old. Having purchased some of the units through the Existing Satisfactory Programme these would not currently meet the Housing Corporation's Development Standards."***

The current climate is difficult for Family First Board members. For example, several years ago when Family First was meeting all Housing Corporation requirements satisfactorily, a member of Family First's Board asked its Housing Corporation Lead Regulator if the Corporation had any adverse comments. He was told everything was fine. Then Family First's rating was announced publicly (internet) on the traffic light assessment as green for viability; green for governance and being properly managed, and amber for development. A Housing Corporation officer told me that this amber assessment was instigated ***"from investment colleagues"***. The Housing Corporation, I then learned, had three strands to its regulation of an association like Family First: investment, lead regulation and financial appraisal. I would have expected the Corporation to answer a Family First Board member's question with one voice.

The Audit Commission now also looks at housing associations on a rolling programme. Family First offered to be one of the pathfinder associations to be visited by the Audit Commission in 2000 because the Chief Executive (Ann Cartwright) felt it had nothing to hide.

When Ann Cartwright first arrived (1997), she said she was treated with suspicion by the Housing Corporation because she was not from a housing background. Her predecessor had worked for the Housing Corporation. She inherited a backlog of largely Housing Corporation-induced finance problems. For example, prior to her arrival, the Housing Corporation had sold on Family First's loan portfolio to a private company

Ann Cartwright said (2005): ***"The deal effectively locked in those registered housing associations who had not taken any steps to adjust their loan portfolio. It appears that Family First took no action around this issue nor does it appear the issue was ever discussed at a Board level . . . In the case of Family First we were locked into 30 and 60-year mortgages with fixed term interest rates ranging from 15% to 7.5% . . . The breakage cost to release them was prohibitive. We did, however, manage to consolidate them a bit and reduce the number of properties tied into the loan. We also managed to lower the interest rates slightly but they are still very high compared to today's rate . . . I don't think the sector tried to resist the move nor does it appear that they complained very much or very loudly. It appears that the National Housing Federation did very little lobbying on the subject – a classic case of the Housing Corporation saying 'Jump' and the sector saying 'How high?' in my view."***

To try to steer the organisation's housing finances on to a firmer footing, for example, Family First did not fully take up a Housing Corporation funding allocation in 2002 to purchase eight four-bedroom houses.

Ann Cartwright told me (2003): ***"We gave the allocation for three of the properties back because, even with the Housing Corporation grant, it was still going to take too long to bring the properties into surplus. If we buy a four-bedroom house, we would have to invest £10,000 - £20,000 bringing it up to the Decent Homes Standard, so it will cost around £120,000+***

"Because Government says housing associations have to equalise their rents down to local authority levels, it is going to take 15-20 years to pay off the loan. Which means, for all that time Family First subsidises it out of the income stream. That's unsustainable."

Such responsible action, however, is interpreted as failing to meet development targets with the consequence of receiving an amber instead of a green light on the regulatory traffic lights system as described above. Then, Housing Corporation managers say they do not place pressure on a housing association!

When I met Housing Corporation managers in 2004, there was some likelihood that housing associations of Family First's size might be placed in a new category for regulatory purposes (as are those with under 250 housing units). That might have allowed it more flexibility. This did not happen.

It is clear that the Housing Act 2004 has again changed the rules dramatically. For instance, by giving power to the Housing Corporation to give social housing grant to non-registered as well as registered social landlords. Will the non-registered social landlords (developers by any other name) be treated to the same degree of regulation as the registered ones? For anyone wishing to get an overview of the complexity of legislation with regard to housing funding, a good place to start is ***An Introductory Guide to Housing Finance in England 2005*** www.cipfa.org.uk/shop.

In Nottingham, there is a now a Regional Housing Board [of the Government's East Midlands Regional Office]. The Housing Corporation is one of a number of participating bodies, as is Nottingham City Council. Strategic decisions about local housing priorities and investment are now taken at this 'top' regional level.

In 2004, when I interviewed Ita Cooke, Manager of Lead Regulators, and Lucie George, Lead Regulator for Family First, at the Housing Corporation offices in Leicester, I tried to find out their view on Family First's role as a small specialist housing association close to the grass roots. I outlined how many previous Family First tenants described their experience as enabling them to rebuild their lives.

Ita Cooke believed that: ***"Family First are better placed than many [housing associations] because they are close to the local community."***

She also told me: ***"Local authorities are keen to have 100% nominations on new developments, whereas we are keen to ensure that associations maintain sustainable communities and that indicates some degree of flexibility about who they are nominating into which properties. That's a real clash."*** Currently, Family First takes 50% Local Authority nominations.

On the question of whether a small association is allowed to survive independently, Lucie George said: ***"We don't push associations into development."*** Ita Cooke agreed: ***"It's nothing we would actually push."***

But she added: ***"In terms of their own development, if they [housing associations] are thinking of expanding, given the changing way that we are looking to invest in organisations, they are unlikely to receive investment through us without entering into some sort of partnership arrangement [e.g. merging with a larger housing association]. So that's something Family First needs to give some thought to if it wants to expand its housing operation.***

"We have got a lot of activity at the moment particularly with the changing investment arrangements. Associations are looking at different forms of partnerships and strategic alliances and I think there are going to be some interesting structures coming out of that. We will remain neutral about those from a regulatory point of view . . . But I would say that it is very time-consuming for associations to explore those routes and I think, if there is a fear, it is a fear that associations take their eye off the ball."

In other words, the demands of bureaucracy inhibit real practical work?

Despite assurances of non-intervention, the Housing Corporation has increasingly placed pressure on housing associations to amalgamate. Family First is now not a preferred partner. It can expect no serious attention from the Housing Corporation in terms of moving its housing work forward. In the past decade, Family First has twice looked into the question of possibly merging with another local housing association. The Board decided against doing so. The issue of creating a strategic alliance is now active again (see Summary).

Non-housing activities

As mentioned earlier in the book, from Family First's start housing was not its only core activity. How does the Housing Corporation view this diversity?

When Family First was required to register with the Housing Corporation after the Housing Act 1974, it was assured that its non-housing activities would be unaffected. As Director at that time, I was told that the Corporation believed Family First's non-housing activities were of positive benefit and should be regarded as one model way in which housing associations might support tenants and others within their neighbourhoods. Examples of non-housing activities were The Croft Family Centre including a 30-place day nursery; practical educational work on housing in two local comprehensive schools; school holiday playschemes; recreational and educational activities for people with mental health issues, and its Furniture and Clothing Service.

At the time of registration, the legal requirements of the Housing Act 1974 stated that a registered housing association should (1) not trade for profit and (2) be established for the purpose of, or have among its objectives or powers those of, providing, constructing, improving or managing either houses for letting or hostels.

There was, therefore, quite clearly no suggestion that other activities were unacceptable.

I was invited to the Corporation's HQ in London on several occasions to speak about Family First as an organisation that offered a practical vision of integrated living within the social housing framework. The then Regional Director for the Corporation's Leicester office was positive and helpful. At that time, Family First's non-housing activities represented over half of its total work.

In 1975, its Management Committee reaffirmed that Family First would remain small, local and bold as it reaffirmed its aims and objectives. Its housing would be developed only at a pace commensurate with its other activities. It continued to find innovative housing solutions not only within its own housing stock. Major growth of social housing units was clearly the role of local authorities and the large housing associations and not that of the small specialist ones. Working close to the grass roots was paramount.

In July 1983, Family First's Director Angus Walker was asked to address the National Federation of Housing Associations' Housing Management Conference on the theme: "Which way housing management?" This was at a time when, he said: ***"Many feel the Government is aiming to squeeze the housing rented sector almost out of existence."*** The pressure was being placed on housing associations to take on wider roles. Whilst he felt wider community services should not be mandatory or undertaken for reasons of expediency, he outlined the work of Family First which had always had a wide range of community services. They encompassed The Croft Family Centre including family support services; Crescent Community Centre; city-wide Furniture Service; three shops, and the Miscellany workshop, a drop-in activities centre. Family First also ran a large training services department. For anyone researching housing associations and their wider role in neighbourhoods, this speech would be worth reading (National Federation of Housing Associations' archive).

I cite the above speech as one instance of how Family First's range of community based projects, which had evolved solely from the needs of the local community, was still being regarded as a successful model in the mid-1980s, almost twenty years after Family First was launched.

Soon after, however, the Housing Corporation's over-prescriptive regulations made that self-help evolution of community services much more difficult.

Today, the Housing Corporation's position bears no relation to those early reassurances and commendation of the value of Family First's non-housing activities. It now assumes the right to decide not only what is appropriate for Family First's portfolio of housing but also the extent of its non-housing activities in which the Housing Corporation has no financial interest. In 2000, correspondence took place between the Housing Corporation and Family First's Chief Executive Ann Cartwright about the extent of Family First's total work that the Housing Corporation would accept as 'non-core'. Ann Cartwright was told in 2001 that before a decision was reached, the Housing Corporation was awaiting the current year's business plan and: ***"Could you also provide us with further clarification of the specific activities of the shops and Kidstuff activities demonstrating their links to specific regeneration initiatives in order for us to form a final view."***

I have yet to understand the Corporation's rationale for regulating matters in which it has no financial/ management interest, providing its own financial input to Family First's housing is well and discretely managed and secured. Housing and non-housing activities are financially separately accounted.

There have been times when the Housing Corporation seriously influenced non-housing decisions in which the Housing Corporation had no stake.

Angus Walker, Director of Family First (1976-1988), says he regretted the separation from Family First of its training work, which became the separate Prospect Training Ltd in 1988, mainly because the Housing Corporation ***"regarded it as being potentially ultra vires . . . Organisationally, I think that it was the wrong thing for Family First to have been forced to do. The irony is that two years later, I was asked to speak at the Housing Corporation's Housing Plus Conference, extolling the virtues of a multi-disciplinary community organisation".***

In my interview with Housing Corporation managers, I asked about the current relationship of the Corporation to Family First's non-housing activities. Ita Cooke said: ***"I think there was a fundamental misunderstanding several years ago when it was perceived [that] we only looked at the housing side and weren't actually interested in the government's arrangements for the whole organisation. I think that that was a major misunderstanding. We have worked better since we have got over that and have explained our role more."***

Lucie George: ***"We [Housing Corporation] used to provide Supported Housing Management Grant. We now provide revenue support for the housing management element of supported housing schemes and other bodies would provide the care funding."***

Ita Cooke: ***"Supporting People***[4] ***arrangements have a major impact on our work, in terms of future viability of organisations. A lot of organisations saw their funding increase in the Supporting People pot, and in the long term we felt that that wasn't a sustainable arrangement. We felt that perhaps Government had underestimated what the likely financial impact was, and now already we are seeing Supporting People teams wanting to cut back the amount of funding . . . We are keeping a close eye on associations that have a high reliance on Supporting People funding."***

These comments were interesting but did not address my query about Family First's non-housing activities. In answer to the direct question: How far do you take other Family First activities into your remit?" I was told: ***"I suppose [Housing Corporation] finance [section] would look at that more closely"*** and: ***"They take an overview as to the impact of those activities and the viability of the organisation."***

Comment

There should be some way that a Government-sponsored body like the Housing Corporation could respect small efficient local housing-plus associations that can be bold and flexible. Out of such schemes, fresh practical thinking and ideas emerge and are tested.

The Housing Corporation's commissioned guide 'Foundations for the future: social, economic and environmental priorities for housing associations' (2002) stated: ***"For housing associations, sustainability is about people choosing to live in housing association property, and being able to support their tenancies. Supporting residents to improve social, economic and physical environment in a way that matters to them helps to keep neighbourhoods desirable."***

These and similar objectives, with which Family First would agree, are stated by the Housing Corporation from time to time. Yet its regulatory processes have undoubtedly systematically thwarted Family First's potential to sustain these objectives.

It is not the fault of particular individual regulators but of an ever-expanding bureaucracy which, at the highest level, has a vested interest in its own survival and proliferation within the context of having to enact the ever-changing ideas of current politicians and their too-often short-term agendas. The financial cost to

[4] Supporting People is a Government programme started in 2003 and sponsored by the Office of the Deputy Prime Minister. It aims 'to bring housing-related support to vulnerable clients' and involves local authorities as agents

society of over-regulation is horrendous. The long-term social cost is immeasurable.

Toward the end of my research for this book (autumn 2005), Family First was seeking a partner housing association. After years of numerous changes (including rent capping, rent convergence and Decent Homes Standard targets) imposed upon the social housing sector, it stated: ***"The recent move to restrict social housing development to a small number of preferred partners has prompted Family First to seek a partner to facilitate its stock-holding growth aspirations.***

"The latest imposed change, the Government's new 'efficiency agenda', means that Family First is also now required to demonstrate year-on-year efficiency savings. This is likely to prove to be increasingly difficult for a small organisation like Family First."

It is fitting to end by quoting a letter (1999) that the Chief Executive, Ann Cartwright, wrote to the Regulations Division of the Housing Corporation concerning the Housing Corporation's consultation Document ***'Regulating Diversity'***.

"Family First was established with the specific belief that some of the most disadvantaged sections of society needed more than a simple roof over their heads: they needed a more holistic range of support and services. To this end and from its inception in 1965, we have set out to provide such a holistic and integrated range of services.

"Over the years, we have been successful in securing funding for our non-housing activities from a variety of sources such as local authorities, health authorities, gifts and donations, direct sales and fees. Whilst remaining a key part of Family First and its identity locally, they operate already as separate cost centres and always have as far as I can tell.

"Our non-housing activities are already heavily monitored and regulated through grant aid agreements and service level agreements by publicly accountable bodies such as Nottingham City Council; Nottinghamshire County Council and the Health Authority. For this reason alone, I fail to see why these activities need further regulation via the Housing Corporation.

"I do not feel the Housing Corporation will have the necessary level of knowledge and understanding to make a judgement of the business case for providing child care services, or parenting skills or mental health services designed to meet the needs of people at a very local level. Especially when the Housing Corporation is not being asked to make any financial contribution to these services.

"Before embarking on any new project, we always make sure that it is financially viable and sustainable. Before the bodies like the Local Authority and/or Health Authority agree to fund any new project they have already examined the business case including the financial viability of the project in great detail. In addition they make sure that there is an exit strategy in place in the event that their funding should cease. So why do we need a further examination by the Housing Corporation? Surely this is a waste of public money and an unnecessary duplication of time and effort and resources.

"I appreciate some of the concerns and reasons behind this consultation paper. However, I feel that the approach to regulation as described in the paper does not recognise and respect the regulatory role of other accountable bodies. I also feel that the creative and innovative talents of organisations like Family First will be severely stifled and restricted and that in the end the only people who will suffer are those most in need: the very people social housing is seeking to target."